Reading Highlights

Jacob Murray

1

WorldCom Edu

Reading Highlights

CONTENTS

On the cover
When Larry Walters was young, he dreamt of being a pilot. He never forgot this dream and one day he took to the skies in a very unusual way. **page 41**

Mike the chicken lost his head, but he never lost his will to survive. Instead of becoming dinner, he became famous! **page 5**

"Human Werewolf Syndrome" sounds scary, but it really isn't. Not everyone who looks like a monster really is one. **page 35**

If machines can wash our clothes, why can't they wash our bodies? The Ultrasonic Bath can—with sound waves! **page 47**

01
U N I T

What's in a Head?

Guesswork

Discuss your answers to these questions with your classmates.

1. What is strange about the picture?

2. Is the chicken alive?

3. Why do you think this photo was taken?

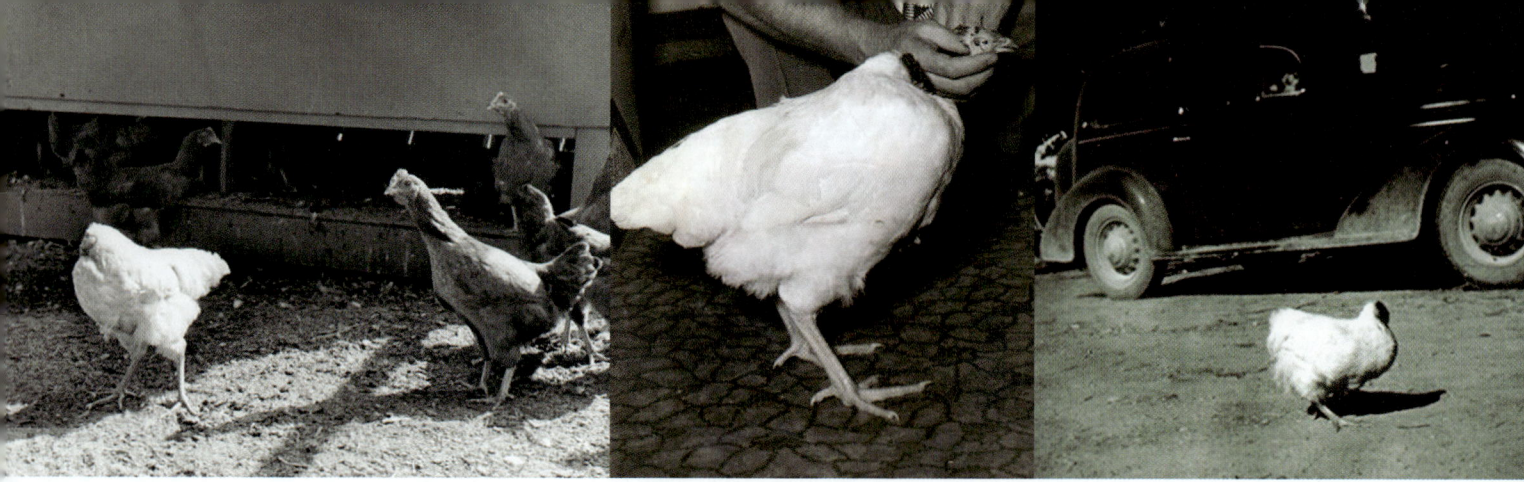

▲ A chicken's heart, lungs and most other body parts are controlled by a small part of its brain that is in the neck. This is how Mike could survive with only a neck!

RH1-01
MP3

What's in a Head?

Mike was a happy chicken. He walked around the yard, and took baths in the dust. At night, he flew up to the perch and slept, just like all the other chickens. Except Mike wasn't like all the other chickens. He was missing one important thing—his head!

Mike wasn't born headless, and his beheading wasn't an accident. It was dinnertime at the Olsen farm, and chicken was on the menu. Farmer Olsen grabbed his sharpest axe and picked out a tasty looking bird. It was Mike. He swung hard and chopped off Mike's head. Mike didn't even fall down! A few minutes later, Mike was walking around and pecking at food with the other chickens. Except he had no head to peck with!

Farmer Olsen expected that Mike would be dead by the next morning. But he woke up to find Mike still alive

▲ In Fruita, Colorado, Mike's birthplace, there is an annual "Mike the Headless Chicken day." Activities include the 5k run, dance, live band and others.

and pecking. Farmer Olsen was so amazed by Mike's survival that he decided to keep Mike alive. For the rest of Mike's life, Farmer Olsen used an eyedropper to feed milk and corn into Mike's neck.

Mike survived this way for a year and a half. Farmer Olsen took "Miracle Mike" on tours around the country, making thousands of dollars. Mike ate so well that he even gained 5 pounds. He was the happiest headless chicken in the world.

▲ When Mike was on tour, he earned close to $4,500 a month — about $50,000 in modern money.

Vocabulary

A. Circle the correct answer and write it in the blank.

1. Dust is dirt that is _____ .

    a. wet   **b.** dry

2. When you behead an animal, you _____ its head.

    a. cut off   **b.** hold up

3. A bird pecks at food with its _____ .

    a. mouth   **b.** feet

4. If you survive an accident, you are _____ .

    a. dead   **b.** alive

5. A perch is a place that is _____ .

    a. high   **b.** low

6. A menu tells you what you can _____ .

    a. eat   **b.** do

B. Write each word in the correct column.

stairs	candy	a finger	a mountain	
hair	clothes	a manhole	a branch	a car

1. pick out

2. fall down

3. chop off

8

Reading Comprehension

A. Main Ideas. Circle the answer that best completes each statement.

1. Mike was different from other chickens because he _____ .

    a. didn't have a head   **b.** took baths in the dust

2. Mike's beheading was _____ .

    a. an accident   **b.** caused by Farmer Olsen

3. Mike was so famous that _____ .

    a. he survived without a head for a year and a half

    b. he made thousands of dollars for Farmer Olsen

B. Details. Circle the answers that best complete each statement.

1. Farmer Olsen (1) _____ , because he wanted to (2) _____ .

(1) **a.** made Mike famous   **b.** chopped Mike's head   **c.** ate Mike's head

(2) **a.** eat Mike for dinner   **b.** become rich   **c.** become famous

2. Even though Mike (1) _____ , he still tried to (2) _____ just like the other chickens.

(1) **a.** was a chicken   **b.** had no head   **c.** looked tasty

(2) **a.** become dinner   **b.** tour the country   **c.** peck at food

C. Inferences. Read each statement and decide if you think it is likely or unlikely. Check the appropriate box.

	Likely	Unlikely
1. Many people paid money to see "Miracle Mike."	☐	☐
2. When Mike finally died, farmer Olsen ate him for dinner.	☐	☐
3. Many chickens survive for a long time after their heads are chopped off.	☐	☐
4. After Mike was beheaded, Farmer Olsen was careful to feed Mike every day.	☐	☐

A. Organize. Write each statement in the correct box.

- A chicken with no head became famous.
- A chicken named Mike
- A headless animal is rare and special.
- Farmer Olsen chopped off Mike's head, but Mike survived.

WHO is the story about?

_____

_____

_____

WHAT happened in the story?

_____

_____

EVENT or topic
"Miracle Mike"

HOW did it happen?

_____

_____

_____

WHY is this event or topic important?

_____

_____

B. Synthesize. Use the chart in Organize above. Fill in the blanks of the advertisement with the correct information.

The World's Freakiest Animals!

When: July 10

Where: The Rochester circus

Featuring "Miracle Mike" the **h**_____ chicken!
A farmer **c**_____ _____ his head, but he **s**_____!
Come and see "**M**_____ _____" and all the other **s**_____ and
r_____ animals yourself!

02
UNIT

Above and Beyond

Guesswork

Discuss your answers to these questions with your classmates.

1. What are the buildings made out of?

2. How long do you think it took to make them?

3. Why do you think the man made these buildings?

◄ The Guinness book of World Records itself holds a world record, as the best-selling copyrighted series of all time. It is also one of the most stolen books from public libraries in the United States.

RH1-02
MP3

Above and Beyond

Do you know how big the largest sandwich in the world is? If you're curious, just check the Guinness Book of World Records. It can tell you about the biggest, smallest, fastest, or greatest of just about anything! The Guinness Book of World Records is so popular that it even set its own record. It is the best-selling copyrighted book ever.

It all started with an argument. Sir Hugh Beaver, the director of Guinness Beer Company, was on a hunting trip. He and the other hunters started arguing about which bird was faster, the golden plover or the grouse. They argued all day, but they never came to an agreement.

▲ Interesting Guinness Records
From ① to ④ : a 4.67-meter-long installation of freestanding playing cards; the world's tallest man, Sultan Kosen (2m 46.5cm); a one kilometer, seven ton piece of gingerbread; a 2,056-kilogram bowl of hummus

That night, Hugh couldn't stop thinking about the argument. He looked in every book he could find, but the answer wasn't anywhere. Right then, he decided that something had to be done. He spoke to the people at Guinness, and they started publishing a book of records. They actually gave it away at first. It became so popular that the next year they sold it in the U.S. It sold 70,000 copies!

Do you have a special talent? Maybe you could set a world record. Age doesn't matter. Arushi Bhatnagar was only 11 months old when she set a world record for being the youngest professional artist ever.

▲ Arushi Bhatnagar was three when she made this painting.

Vocabulary

A. Answer the questions in complete sentences. The first one has been done for you.

1. The boys had an argument during lunch. Did they agree or disagree?

They disagreed.

2. You can't copy that movie. It is copyrighted. Is it protected or unprotected?

_____

3. Marie has a talent for playing the tuba. Is she skilled or unskilled?

_____

4. The company's director is a very kind and understanding person. Is she a follower or a leader?

_____

5. Trevor is curious about what it is like to travel in space. Does Trevor want to know more or less about space?

_____

6. Usain Bolt holds world records for three different races. Is this normal or incredible?

_____

B. Read the passage below. Match each phrase in red with its equivalent expression.

Who ever said that size **wasn't important**? Not the people of Thomas Kemper Soda Company. They **decided** to make a giant root beer float! They took a huge tank and filled it with 300 gallons of ice cream and 2,000 gallons of soda. Then they **donated** the treat to a very thirsty audience!

1. gave away _____

2. didn't matter _____

3. came to an agreement _____

A. Main Ideas. Complete the statement by circling the correct choice for each blank.

The passage is mainly about the **1.** _____ of **2.** _____ . So the main idea is that **3.** _____ .

1. a. origins   **b.** success

2. a. Sir Hugh Beaver   **b.** Guinness Book of World Records

3. a. the Guinness Book of World Records got started with a single question by Sir Hugh
   b. Sir Hugh made a great success by publishing the Guinness Book of World Records

B. Details. Circle the correct answer for each question.

1. The hunters started arguing because _____ .

   a. the Guinness book of records was wrong
   b. the grouse was faster than the golden plover
   c. they didn't agree about which bird was faster

2. How did the Guinness Book of World Records change after the first publication?

   a. It had fewer records.
   b. It started costing money.
   c. It was published all over the world.

C. Inferences. Decide which of the statements can be inferred from the passage. Check the correct answers. (Choose two.)

_____ **1.** The Guinness Book of World Records is sold in every country in the world.

_____ **2.** Guinness made a lot of money selling the Guinness Book of World Records.

_____ **3.** Guinness only accepts world records from very young people.

_____ **4.** Many people buy the Guinness Book of World Records every year.

Writing

A. Organize. Complete this diagram to show the history of The Guinness Book of World Records.

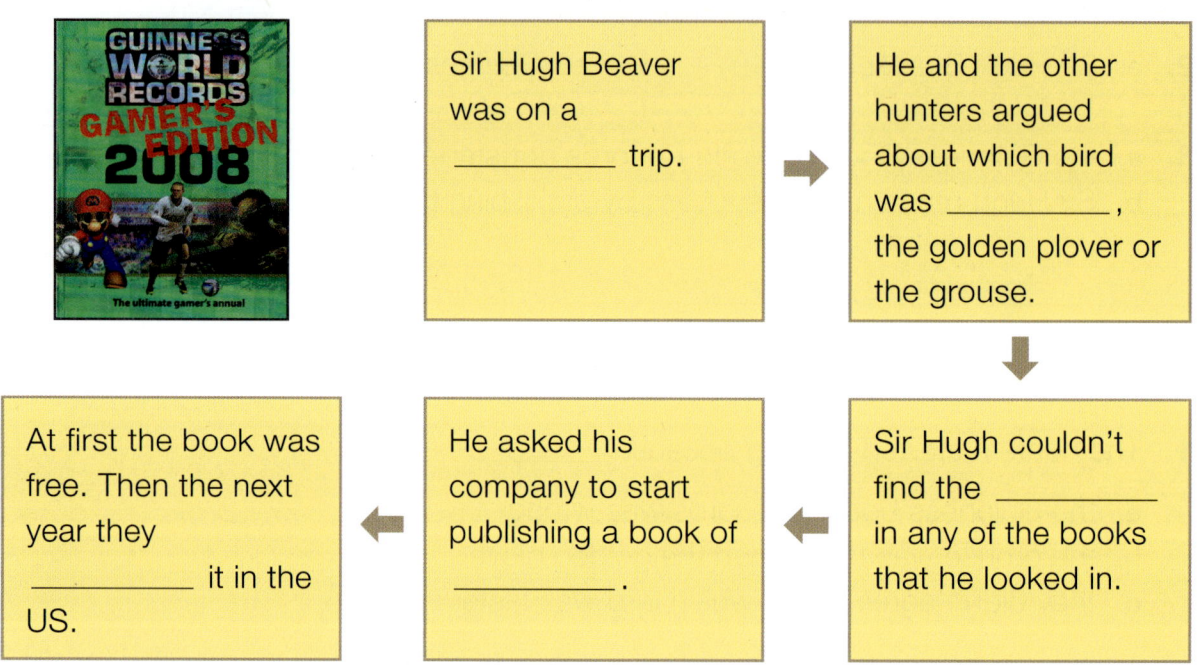

How the Guinness Book of World Records Got Started

Sir Hugh Beaver was on a _____ trip.

He and the other hunters argued about which bird was _____, the golden plover or the grouse.

Sir Hugh couldn't find the _____ in any of the books that he looked in.

He asked his company to start publishing a book of _____.

At first the book was free. Then the next year they _____ it in the US.

B. Synthesize. Using the chart in Organize above, complete the conversation between Sir Hugh Beaver and a reporter.

Reporter: Where did you get the idea for The Guinness Book of World Records?

Sir Hugh: It started with a question. _____ (3words), the golden plover or the grouse?

Reporter: Could you find the answer?

Sir Hugh: No, it wasn't in any books.

Reporter: So you asked Guinness to _____ (5words)?

Sir Hugh: Yes, _____ (3words) at first, but the next year they sold it in the U.S.

03
U N I T

A Surprise from the Sky

Guesswork

Discuss your answers to these questions with your classmates.

1. What is happening in this picture? What are the people trying to do?

2. Why do you think so many whales are lying on the beach?

3. Do you think the whales beached themselves on purpose?

▲ Jatinga — the valley of Birds

▲ A bird lover releasing a bird in Jatinga

India

RH1-03
MP3

A Surprise from the Sky

Raju waited patiently on a cliff in Jatinga, India. It was a dark, moonless night, and there was a thick fog. Raju could barely see. He didn't mind, though. He was looking for food and the darkness was perfect.

Suddenly, Raju heard a soft sound in the darkness. He moved his torch towards the sound. There was a dead bird on the ground. Raju picked it up and put it in his bag.

▲ The birds of Jatinga only fall from the sky between the hours of 7 and 11 at night. Some people think that the birds mistakenly fly towards the villagers' torches on the ground.

▲ There is a special building for watching the birds of Jatinga. Tourists can stay there and see the phenomenon themselves. The mystery of Jatinga is not limited to one kind of bird. Many different kinds of birds fall from the sky all over Jatinga.

Then there was another sound, and then another. Raju moved the torch and looked. There were more birds on the ground. They were falling out of the sky! Raju was happy. His family would eat well tonight.

Every fall, a strange thing happens in the village of Jatinga. On certain dark and foggy nights, birds mysteriously fall from the sky. No one knows exactly why this happens. Early villagers thought that the birds were spirits sent from the sky to scare them. Modern villagers are less superstitious. They often eat the fallen birds.

One theory is that the birds are confused by the fog and the dark. But other places in the world are foggy and dark too. Why don't birds fall from the sky all over the world? It may always be a mystery. The villagers don't mind, though. They're just happy to live in such a special place!

Vocabulary

A. Fill in each blank with the correct adjective from the word box.

mysterious	moonless	foggy	modern	
superstitious	certain	patient	perfect	soft

1. Mike waited a long time for me to finish my lunch. He was very _____ .

2. A man left this _____ present for me. I don't know who he was!

3. Ancient people brushed their teeth with twigs. _____ people use toothbrushes.

4. Daniel is too _____ . He thinks that black cats are bad luck!

5. That pillow is too _____ . I sleep better with a hard pillow.

6. Not all diamonds are _____ .

7. _____ weather can sometimes be more dangerous for drivers than snow.

8. _____ nights are the best to watch the stars.

9. _____ colors are known to change your feelings.

B. Draw lines to make correct sentences. Write the completed sentences below.

1. She picked up •   • if you •   • and hit her brother with it.

2. I don't mind •   • a window •   • eat my pizza.

3. You fell out of •   • a stick •   • and hit the ground.

(1) She picked up _____

(2) I don't mind _____

(3) You fell out of _____

A. Main Ideas. Circle the answer that best completes each statement.

1. Raju's story shows _____ .

    a. why the birds fall from the sky

    b. how the villagers feel about the birds falling from the sky

2. A modern theory about the falling birds is that _____ .

    a. they are confused by the fog and the dark

    b. they fall all over the world, but are only seen in Jatinga

B. Details. Write True or False after each statement.

1. Raju used the torch to find the dead birds. _____

2. Birds fall from the sky over Jatinga every year. _____

3. Modern villagers can stop the birds from falling. _____

4. Raju was happy because he found food for his family. _____

C. Inferences. Based on your understanding of the text, choose the best way to complete each of these statements.

1. Raju probably _____ .

    a. ate bird for dinner all year

    b. ate bird for dinner only a few times a year

2. Early villagers probably _____ .

    a. ate the birds after they fell

    b. stayed inside when the birds fell

3. Modern villagers probably _____ .

    a. don't care about solving the mystery of Jatinga

    b. try hard to solve the mystery of Jatinga

Writing

A. Organize. Look at the outline of the main ideas in the passage. Fill in the details that illustrate these main ideas. Choose from the list of details.

- Some people think the birds are confused by the dark and the fog.
- Modern villagers aren't superstitious.
- Villagers eat the fallen birds.
- Other places in the world are dark and foggy.

OUTLINE	
Main Ideas	**Details**
1. Villagers enjoy the mystery of Jatinga.	a. _____ b. _____ _____
2. The birds of Jatinga may always be a mystery.	a. _____ _____ b. _____ _____

B. Synthesize. Use the chart in Organize above. Complete the conversation between Raju and a reporter.

Reporter:	How do you feel about the mystery of the falling birds?
Raju:	I like it. It brings food for my family.
Reporter:	You mean that you eat the **f**_____ **b**_____?
Raju:	Yes, we do. We're not **s**_____ like early villagers were.
Reporter:	Do you know why the birds fall on Jatinga?
Raju:	Some people think that they are **c**_____ by the dark and the **f**_____.
Reporter:	What do you think?
Raju:	I think other places are dark and **f**_____. So why is Jatinga special?

04

U N I T

A Flying Trap

Guesswork

Discuss your answers to these questions with your classmates.

1. Count the dragonfly's legs. What is it using them for?

2. What other things could a dragonfly use its legs for?

3. What part of the dragonfly do you think is most important for catching prey?

▲ A dragonfly eating a small blue butterfly

RH1-04
MP3

A Flying Trap

Have you ever seen a dragonfly? Their big wings and brightly colored bodies make them easy to spot. If you're lucky, one might land on you. If that happens, take a close look at it. You might be surprised by what you see.

Dragonfly larva

Dragonfly emerging
from larval stage

Adult dragonfly

▲ A dragonfly larva breathes through
its butt! It can also use its bottom to
push water out and move itself
through water.

▲ Some large dragonflies live for up to
5 years as larva. Their adult lives are
relatively short: only 5 to 6 months.

The first things you'll notice are its big wings. Without them, a dragonfly would be helpless. Its wings let it move in 6 different directions: up, down, forwards, backwards, left, and right. Not only that, but it can fly up to 50 or 60 miles per hour. Even helicopters can't fly that well.

With such powerful wings, you might think a dragonfly has no use for legs, but that isn't exactly true. Like all insects, dragonflies have six legs. But dragonflies are a bit different. They don't use their legs for walking. They use them to catch prey.

A dragonfly feeds on smaller insects, and it catches them while it is flying. Each of its legs is covered in tiny hairs. Together the legs form a hairy trap. They hang beneath the dragonfly, sort of like a spider's web, except this trap doesn't wait for prey to find it. It finds the prey!

Dragonflies spend most of their time hunting with their hairy legs. They need to hunt a lot, as some smaller dragonflies live for only a few weeks!

Did You Know?

In Japan, children catch dragonflies as a game. They throw a hair with small pebbles tied to it into the air. The dragonfly thinks it's an insect and gets tangled up!

Vocabulary

A. Circle the answer that fits best with the word in red.

1. bright   sun / clouds / ocean

2. form   break / make / lake

3. direction   up / about / somewhat

4. insect   shrimp / fly / mouse

5. beneath   above / under / beside

6. powerful   weak / heavy / strong

7. prey   food / hunter / vegetable

8. spot   listen / touch / see

9. catch   trap / release / move

10. notice   help / bring / see

B. Fill in the blanks using the expressions from the box.

have no use for	sort of	feed on	take a close look at

1. Here, _____ my shirt. Can you see the coffee stain?

2. I _____ expensive shoes and clothes. I work outside every day.

3. Your hat looks _____ like a squirrel. Is it supposed to look like that?

4. Some insects, like the praying mantis, _____ their own kind.

Reading Comprehension

A. Main Ideas. Circle the correct answer for each question.

1. Which part of a dragonfly is most important for movement?

    a. wings

    b. legs

2. What helps a dragonfly's legs catch prey?

    a. their size

    b. their hair

3. How are a dragonfly's legs like a spider web?

    a. They trap prey.

    b. They wait for prey.

B. Details. Write Opinion or Fact after each statement.

1. It is lucky if a dragonfly lands on you.   _____

2. A dragonfly cannot survive without its wings.   _____

3. Most people think a dragonfly's legs are useless.   _____

4. Some dragonflies live for only a short period of time.   _____

C. Inferences. Decide which of the statements can be inferred from the passage. Check the correct answers. (Choose one.)

_____ **1.** Dragonflies are good hunters.

_____ **2.** Dragonflies are bad luck in some cultures.

_____ **3.** Dragonflies are hunted by other insects.

_____ **4.** Many places have a problem with too many dragonflies.

A. Organize. Write each fact in the correct box.

a. live for only a few weeks   b. large and powerful

c. covered with tiny hairs   d. used to catch prey

e. help to move in many directions   f. brightly colored

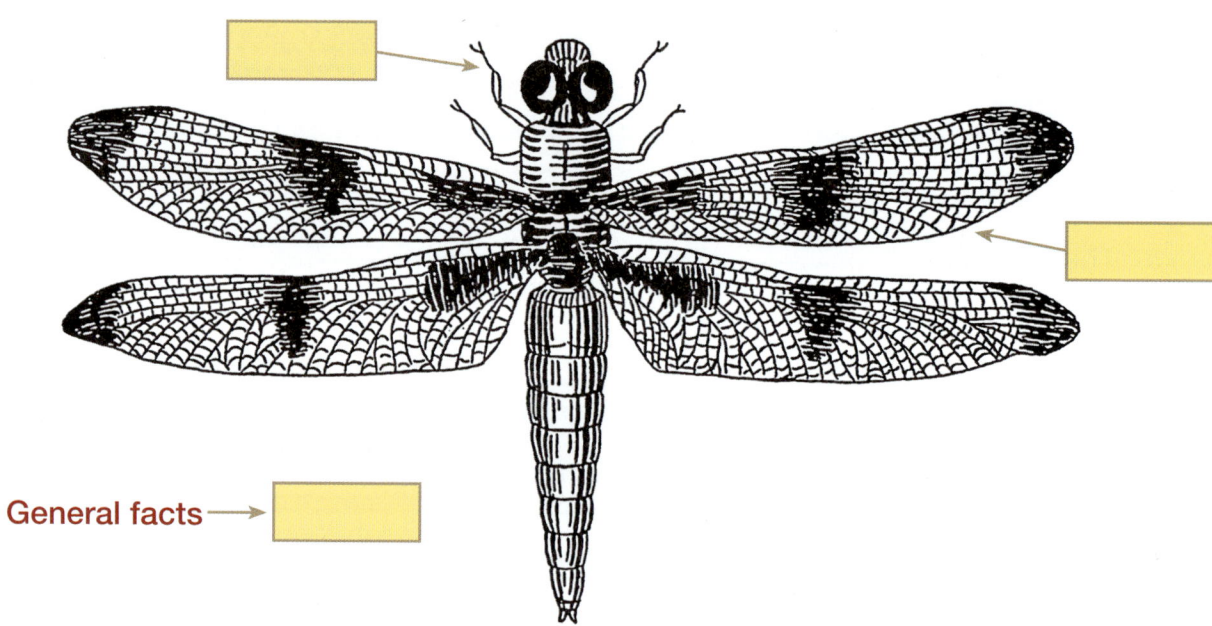

General facts →

B. Synthesize. Consider the information provided in Organize above. Complete each sentence.

1. Dragonflies use their _____ and _____ wings to help them move in _____ _____ _____ .

2. A dragonfly's legs are covered with _____ _____ that are used to _____ _____ .

3. A dragonfly's _____ _____ body makes it easy to spot.

4. Dragonflies don't have much time to hunt. They live for only _____ _____ _____ .

UNIT

A Different Kind of Brain

Guesswork

Discuss your answers to these questions with your classmates.

1. What is the man doing?

2. Does he seem strange at all? Why?

3. Can you guess what his special talent is?

RH1-05
MP3

A Different Kind of Brain

How many books have you read? Can you remember all the titles? How about all the words? Kim Peek could. He could remember every word of at least 12,000 different books. That's like having a library in your head.

Kim Peek was born with a rare disease. He didn't learn to walk until he was four, and he could never button his shirt. He was also slow to learn many important social skills. Kim's disease wasn't all bad, though.

Kim's brain was like a sponge. His father said that he started memorizing books when he was just over one year old. He didn't read like most people. He'd read two pages at once, one page with each eye! And each page only took about eight seconds.

Kim's story was so amazing that a movie was made about it. After the movie became popular, Kim gained a lot of confidence. He would go up to people and ask their birthday. Then he would tell them what day of the week they were born on. He could even tell them what stories were in the newspaper on that day.

Sadly, Kim died in 2009 of a heart attack, so you will never get to meet this incredible man in person. But if you're curious, you can always watch the movie about his life.

RAIN MAN
ORIGINAL MOTION PICTURE
SOUNDTRACK

▲ Kim Peek with Barry Morrow, screenwriter for Rain Man, holding one of the Oscars awarded for the film (left); The movie made about Kim Peek was called "Rain Man." It is a fun and loving look at Kim's amazing life.

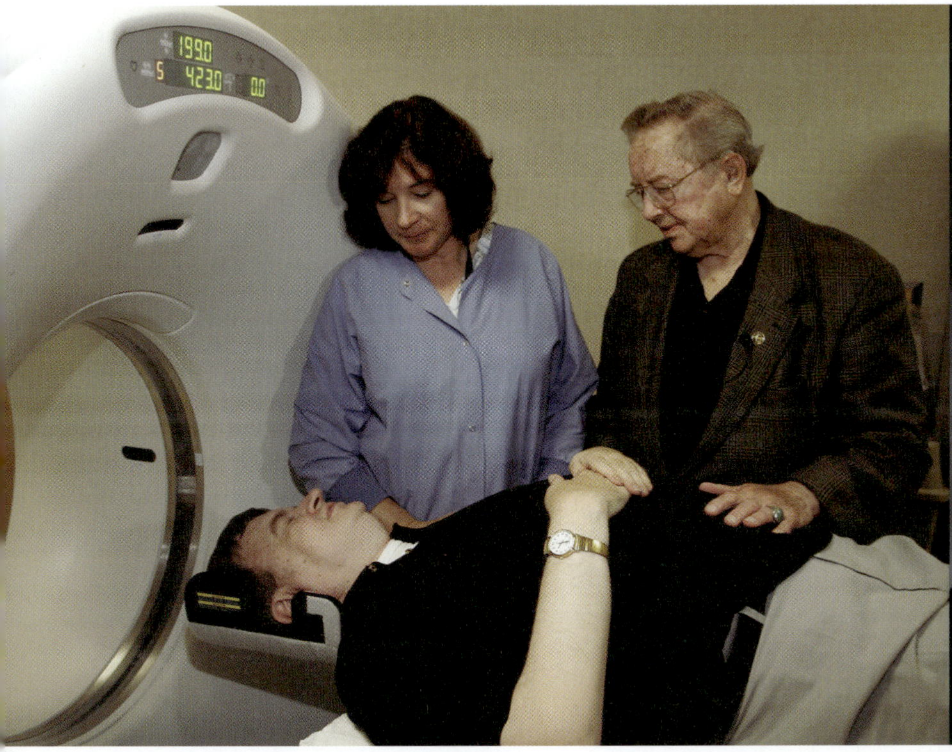

▲ Later, scientists found out that Kim Peek was missing his corpus callosum—the part that connects the two halves of the brain together.

▲ **Kim Peek (left) and his father Fran Peek** Kim's father said that when Kim was a child he would read a book in about an hour, and he remembered almost everything he had read.

Vocabulary

A. Answer each question in a complete sentence. The first one has been done for you.

1. Diamonds are rare gems. Are they common or uncommon?

They are uncommon.

2. My trip to Thailand was incredible! Was the trip amazing or boring?

_____

3. I use a sponge to clean the dishes. Does the sponge hold air or water?

_____

4. Mary has a disease that makes her cough a lot. Is she sick or healthy?

_____

5. I can't decide on a title for my book. Am I thinking of a name or a design?

_____

6. When I was twelve, I memorized a poem by Shakespeare. Did I forget or remember the poem?

_____

B. Read the passage below. Match each phrase in red with its equivalent expression.

When I was young, a man **approached** me and asked if I wanted some ice cream. I said yes and I tried all the flavors **at the same time**. It was **a bit more than** I could eat and I got sick afterwards!

1. at once   _____

2. just over   _____

3. came up to   _____

Reading Comprehension

A. Main Ideas. Complete the statement by circling the correct choice for each blank.

The passage is mainly about the **1.** _____ of a **2.** _____ man. So the main idea is that **3.** _____ .

1. a. struggle   **b.** success

2. a. common   **b.** special

3. a. because of his disease Kim Peek suffered a lot
b. because of his disease Kim Peek was able to do some amazing things

B. Details. Complete each sentence with the correct answer.

1. Kim Peek's brain was like a library because _____ .

   a. it held a lot of information   **b.** it was very quiet and peaceful

2. Kim's disease made it difficult for him to _____ .

   a. remember important dates   **b.** deal with other people

3. Kim read books differently from other people by _____ .

   a. reading each page with both eyes   **b.** memorizing each page with a different eye

4. Once Kim gained confidence, he started telling strangers _____ .

   a. amazing facts about themselves   **b.** amazing things about his life

C. Inferences. Read each statement and decide if you think it is likely or unlikely. Check the appropriate box.

	Likely	Unlikely
1. Kim Peek never saw the movie about his life.	☐	☐
2. Kim needed help with many everyday things.	☐	☐
3. Kim felt really bad about his disease.	☐	☐
4. Kim Peek could remember the author of every book he had ever read.	☐	☐

Writing

A. Organize. Place each detail in the correct box. Some boxes may be left empty.

    a. slow to learn social skills

    b. could never button shirt

    c. slow to learn to walk

    d. memorized at least 12,000 books

    e. read using one eye for each page

    f. told strangers newspaper stories from the day they were born

    g. gained confidence after movie became popular

	GOOD	BAD
Social Skills		
Memory		
Physical abilities (e.g. combing hair, tying shoes…)		

B. Synthesize. Use the chart in Organize above. Fill in the blanks of the advertisement with the correct information.

"Rain Man"

A loving story about an amazing man with a unique disease.

He struggled with normal things. He could

_____ .
    (Describe physical abilities)

And he was _____ .
                (Describe social skills)

But he could do some incredible things. He _____ , and he
                                                      (Describe memory)

could even tell strangers newspaper stories _____ !
                                                         (Describe memory)

Come watch the movie and be amazed!

06

A Beastly Disease

Discuss your answers to these questions with your classmates.

1. What is strange about this young girl?

2. Do you think this is a picture of a real person?

3. What problems might the person in this picture face?

One mild form of hypertrichosis is called hirsutism. It causes some women to grow soft hair on their faces. The hair is easily removed, though.

A Beastly Disease

RH1-06
MP3

Werewolves are fearsome monsters. Most of the time they appear to be normal people. But once a month, when the moon is full, something terrible happens. Their hair grows long and they become dangerous, bloodthirsty beasts. Luckily werewolves are just a myth. Or are they?

The legend of the werewolf may have its origins in truth. There is a disease called hypertrichosis, also known as werewolf syndrome. It can cause people to look like beasts. People with hypertrichosis aren't werewolves, and they definitely aren't bloodthirsty. But their hair does grow, and not just during a full moon. For their entire lives, they are often covered from head to toe with long, thick hair.

In the past, people with hypertrichosis suffered greatly. Not from the long hair itself, but because they looked strange. This made it difficult to find work. Instead of normal jobs, these people often ended up in circuses. They stayed in cages all day, while circus-goers pointed and laughed at them like they were beasts.

Larry Ramos Gomez has hypertrichosis, a condition which causes his body to produce excessive facial and torso hair.

A bearded lady from a travelling circus

Julia Pastrana was a well-known circus performer from the 1800s. She was known as "the bearded lady." She had hair all over, even on the palms of her hands!

Now we know that werewolves don't exist, and that people with strange diseases, like hypertrichosis, need to be treated like anybody else. Luckily modern science helps as well. Most people with werewolf syndrome can just have the hair removed. No one has to look like a beast if they don't want to!

Petrus Gonzales and his daughter
The first recorded case of hypertrichosis was Petrus Gonzales in 1648. Many of his children and grandchildren also suffered from hypertrichosis.

A. Circle the correct answer to each question and write it in the blank.

1. A myth is a story that is _____ .

    a. fact   **b.** fiction

2. An invention's origin is its _____ .

    a. beginning   **b.** end

3. A syndrome is a kind of _____ .

    a. growth   **b.** disease

4. To suffer is to feel _____ .

    a. pleasure   **b.** pain

5. A cage is used to _____ creatures.

    a. free   **b.** trap

6. To remove a sticker is to _____ .

    a. take it off   **b.** put it on

B. Draw lines to make correct sentences. Write the completed sentences below.

1. I don't want to •   • is known as •   • "Silly Sally" because •   • that is rude.

2. My friend Sally •   • end up in •   • strangers because •   • I study hard.

3. We never   •   • laugh at •   • a bad school so •   • she laughs a lot.

(1) I don't want to _____

(2) My friend Sally _____

(3) We never _____

A. Main Ideas. Circle the answer that best completes each statement.

1. This passage is mainly about _____ .

    a. a strange disease

    b. bloodthirsty beasts

2. Hypertrichosis is called werewolf syndrome because it _____ .

    a. causes people to grow long hair

    b. makes people change during a full moon

3. People with hypertrichosis often had to work at circuses because _____ .

    a. the disease was so painful

    b. they looked strange

B. Details. Write True or False after each statement.

1. Hypertrichosis may explain the origins of the myth about werewolves. _____

2. Werewolves turn into people when the moon is full. _____

3. Hypertrichosis causes people to turn into beasts. _____

4. People with hypertrichosis often found jobs at the circus. _____

5. At the circus, people with hypertrichosis stayed in cages all day. _____

C. Inferences. Decide which of the statements can be inferred from the passage. Check the correct answers. (Choose three.)

_____ **1.** In the past, people with hypertrichosis were often treated poorly.

_____ **2.** Now, many people with hypertrichosis look just like anybody else.

_____ **3.** In the past, people with hypertrichosis often lived with animals.

_____ **4.** Now, many people with hypertrichosis have normal jobs.

Writing

A. Organize. Write each answer (a-h) in the correct place in the chart.

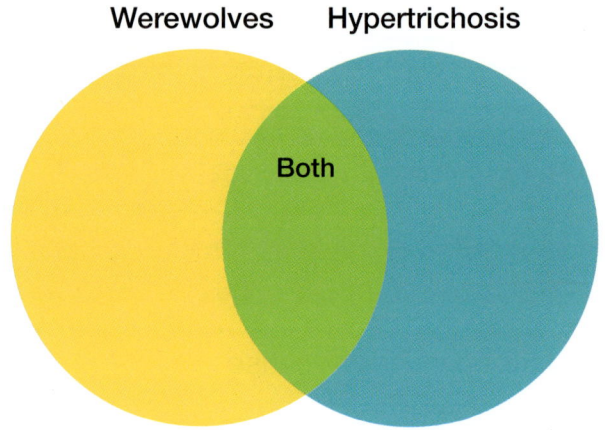

Werewolves   Hypertrichosis

Both

a. grow long hair
b. change during the full moon
c. work at a circus
d. bloodthirsty beasts
e. stay in cages all day
f. helped by modern science
g. an old legend
h. look like a beast

B. Synthesize. Use the chart in Organize above. Complete the conversation between Julia Pastrana and a reporter.

Reporter:	When did you find out that you had hypertrichosis?
Julia:	When I was young. I started _____ all over my body. That's when I knew. *(What happened to your body?)*
Reporter:	How did you feel about it?
Julia:	It was horrible. I thought that I _____. *(What did you look like?)*
Reporter:	How about when you grew up? Did it get better?
Julia:	Well, I _____. *(Where did you work?)*
Reporter:	How was that?
Julia:	It wasn't much better. They made me _____ all day long! *(Where did you stay?)*

07
U N I T

Reach for the Sky

Guesswork

Discuss your answers to these questions with your classmates.

1. What is happening in the photo?

2. Where is the man going to go?

3. Why do you think this flying machine was created?

▲ Kent Couch launching his custom-made, cluster balloon lawn chair from Bend, Oregon

RH1-07
MP3

Reach for the Sky

When he was a kid, Larry Walters dreamed of being a pilot. Sadly, because of poor eyesight, Larry was forced to give up his dream. He never forgot about flying, though. Years later, he finally took to the skies — in a flying chair!

Larry first had the idea of a flying chair when he was 13. He saw weather balloons in a shop. He wondered if they could lift him into the sky. 20 years later, Larry decided to give it a try! He bought 45 weather balloons and tied them to a lawn chair. He packed sandwiches, cold beer, a camera and a pellet gun for the ride. Then he strapped himself into the chair, and he was off.

He only planned to float about 30 feet above his backyard. But his plans quickly changed. The balloons were so strong that they snapped the rope that was holding him down. Larry quickly rose to about 15,000 feet — that's higher than most mountains. Larry was fine, but then he started drifting toward an airport runway. He didn't want to get hit by a plane!

▲ lawn chair

▲ In July 2007, Kent Couch, a 48-year-old gas station owner, flew 193 miles in a homemade aircraft made of a chair and 105 colorful rubber balloons. For his next flight Couch spent about 9 hours in the air and traveled around 240 miles. Kent also holds an unofficial world record for "highest altitude reached" at 16,625 feet.

Larry knew he had to act quickly. He shot a few balloons with his pellet gun, and started slowly floating down. When he finally landed, Larry was quickly arrested. Larry wasn't too worried, though. He'd just realized his childhood dream.

Did You Know?
When Larry landed, his chair got tangled in power lines. This caused a 20 minute blackout for much of the area.

❝It was something I had to do. I had this dream for twenty years, and if I hadn't done it, I think I would have ended up in the funny farm. I didn't think that by fulfilling my goal in life-my dream-that I would create such a stir and make people laugh.❞ ▶

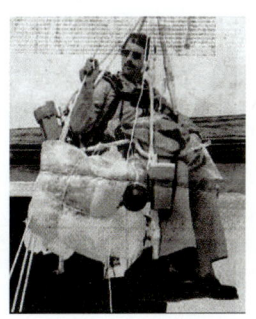

Vocabulary

A. Circle the answer that fits best with the word in red.

1. **pilot**   sky / earth / ocean

2. **lift**   down / up / forwards

3. **tie**   string / chair / tree

4. **pack**   seat / bag / stairs

5. **lawn**   dirt / rocks / grass

6. **pellet gun**   shoot / throw / crush

7. **runway**   building / road / statue

8. **snap**   break / make / take

9. **float**   coin / boat / car

10. **balloon**   square / triangle / circle

B. Fill in the blanks using the expressions from the box.

because of	give it a try	holding down	took to the sky

1. Those rocks are _____ the blanket. If you take them, it will blow away!

2. You've never eaten sushi. You should _____ .

3. I lost my glasses _____ you. I'm very angry.

4. I ran through the pigeons, and they all _____ .

Reading Comprehension

A. Main Ideas. Complete the statement by circling the correct choice for each blank.

The passage is mainly about the **1.** _____ of **2.** _____ . So the main idea is that **3.** _____ .

1. a. childhood dream   **b.** sudden arrest

2. a. a pilot   **b.** a regular man

3. a. Larry Walters realized his childhood dream by floating into the sky in a chair
   b. Larry Walters became a pilot by dreaming about flying in a chair

B. Details. Circle the correct answer for each question.

1. Why didn't Larry become a pilot?

   a. because he grew too old   **b.** because he couldn't see well

2. How old was Larry when he took to the skies in a flying chair?

   a. 20   **b.** 33

3. How high did Larry first plan on flying?

   a. 30 feet   **b.** 15,000 feet

4. What was Larry worried about after he flew too high?

   a. being hit by a plane   **b.** being arrested

C. Inferences. Read each statement and decide if you think it is likely or unlikely. Check the appropriate box.

	Likely	Unlikely
1. Many people were amazed by Larry's flight.	☐	☐
2. Larry took the pellet gun so he could shoot birds.	☐	☐
3. Larry didn't know how strong the weather balloons would be.	☐	☐
4. Larry planned on being in the sky for a while.	☐	☐

Writing

A. Organize. Number the pictures in order to show the history of Larry Walters' incredible flight.

 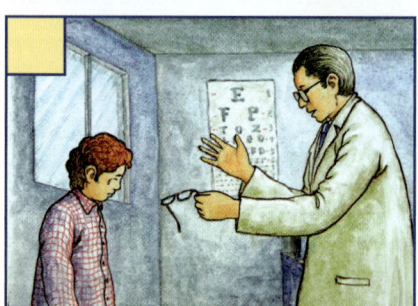

B. Synthesize. Look at the pictures in Organize above. Complete the diagram.

How Larry Walters Took to the Sky

As a kid, Larry dreamed of being a _____ , but couldn't because of poor _____ .

⬇

At age 13, Larry had the idea of a _____ _____ after seeing weather _____ in a shop.

⬇

20 years later, Larry tied 45 weather _____ to a _____ _____ and floated into the sky.

⬇

After he reached 15,000 feet, Larry _____ some balloons and started floating down.

⬇

Finally, Larry realized his childhood dream.

Though it was thought to be an incredible invention when it first came out, the automatic human washing machine is still not available for purchase.

08

The Clean Machine

Guesswork

Discuss your answers to these questions with your classmates.

1. Can you imagine what this machine is used for?

2. Why do you think it was invented?

3. How do you think it works?

The Clean Machine

Getting dirty is easy, but getting clean can take time. Clothes, cars, dishes and people all need regular washing. In the past, people would spend hours a day cleaning their things. Now, we have machines that will do the job for us. They'll clean almost anything imaginable, from shoes to skyscrapers. But what about a machine that cleans people?

Soon showers may be a thing of the past. The human washing machine is here, and it may be coming to you soon! It's called the Ultrasonic Bath, and it can clean and dry a person in less than 15 minutes. It's as simple as washing clothes. You just climb into the machine and press a button. The Ultrasonic Bath does the rest.

The key to the Ultrasonic Bath is sound. Have you ever seen thunder shake a building? Sound can be powerful. The bath fills with water, and then sends sound waves through the water at your body. The sound vibrates the dirt right off of you.

There's no need for a towel, either. When you're all clean, the Ultrasonic Bath dries you with jets of hot air. When you're dry, just climb out of the Ultrasonic Bath and you'll be feeling like a new person. If only it could dress you, too!

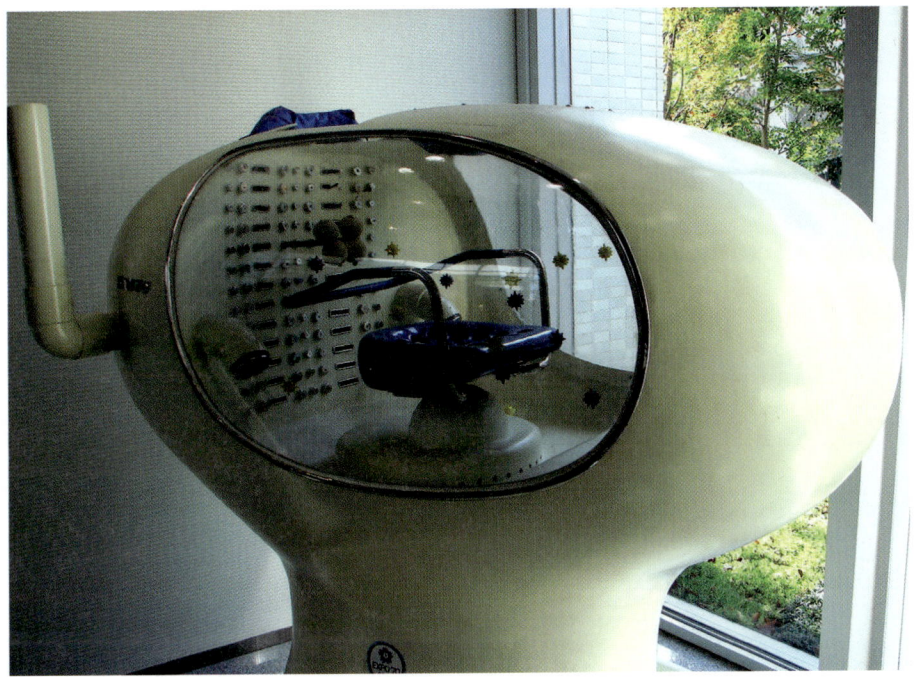

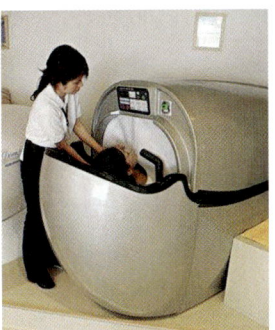

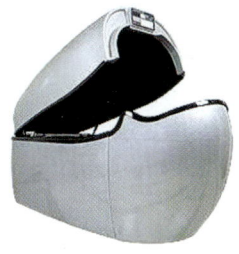

▲ The Ultrasonic Bath was first displayed at the 1970 World Expo in Osaka, Japan. It was created by electronics maker, Sanyo.

▲ Santelubain 999(avant): an automatic cleaning mechanism which shampoos your body, plays music and provides aromatherapy

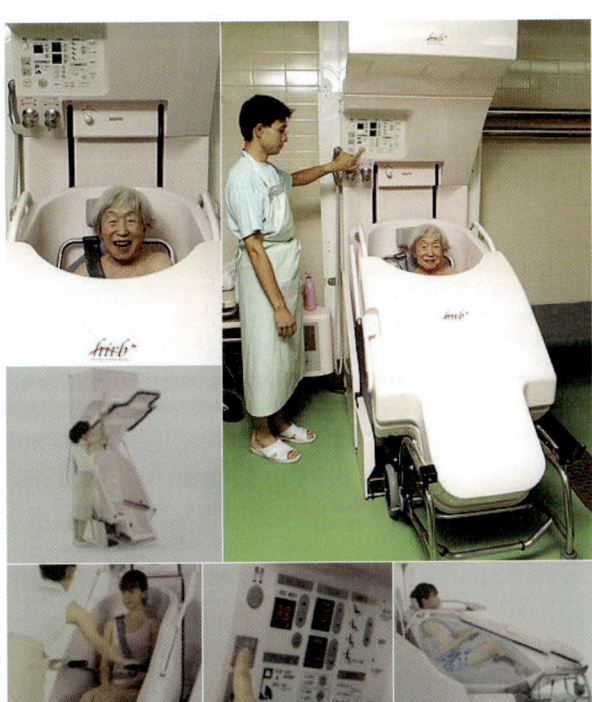

▲ The Ultrasonic Bath is not yet available for in-home use, but a version called the HIRB (short for harmony in roll-lo bathing, because people are rolled into it) is being used in some Japanese elderly homes. With the HIRB you still have to dry yourself, though!

▲ People who have used the Ultrasonic Bath report that it tickles the skin, and leaves you feeling nice and warm, but not too hot.

Vocabulary

A. Answer the questions in complete sentences. The first one has been done for you.

1. HIV is a human disease. Does it affect people or animals?

   It affects people.

2. My aunt used to live at the top of a skyscraper. Was her building tall or short?

   _____

3. There are many types of ultrasonic cleaners. Do they use lasers or sound?

   _____

4. You can start some cars by pressing a button. Do you push or turn the button?

   _____

5. That storm had some incredible thunder. Did I see the thunder or hear it?

   _____

6. My mother still has to dress my brother in the morning. Does she put on or take off his clothes for him?

   _____

B. Read the passage below. Match each phrase in red with its equivalent expression.

In the future, cars might be **old-fashioned**. We won't have to **enter** or **exit** vehicles anymore. There will just be a big tube that carries you wherever you want to go!

1. climb into   _____

2. a thing of the past   _____

3. climb out of   _____

Reading Comprehension

A. Main Ideas. Circle the correct answer for each question.

1. How do cleaning machines make life easier?

    a. They save us time.

    b. They save us money.

2. How is the Ultrasonic Bath different from regular cleaning machines?

    a. It cleans faster and better.

    b. It cleans people.

3. What doesn't the Ultrasonic Bath do for you?

    a. dry you off

    b. put your clothes on

B. Details. Write True or False after each statement.

1. The Ultrasonic Bath can also be used for washing clothes. _____

2. A person can start the Ultrasonic Bath by making sound. _____

3. The sound waves move through the water and knock the dirt off of you. _____

4. The Ultrasonic Bath uses jets of hot air to dry you. _____

5. Scientists are working on a machine that will dress you too. _____

C. Inferences. Decide which of the statements can be inferred from the passage. Check the correct answers. (Choose two.)

_____ **1.** The Ultrasonic Bath will be cheap to buy.

_____ **2.** Sound can be used to clean things other than people as well.

_____ **3.** The Ultrasonic Bath can clean you while you are wearing clothes.

_____ **4.** The Ultrasonic Bath could be useful for people who can't use their legs.

Writing

A. Organize. Write each statement in the correct box.

• It uses sound to vibrate dirt right off of you.
• You climb in and press a button.
• A human washing machine.
• It cleans and dries a person in less than 15 minutes.

WHAT is the story about?

_____
_____
_____

WHAT does it do?

_____
_____
_____

EVENT or topic

"The Ultrasonic Bath"

HOW do you start it?

_____
_____
_____

HOW does it work?

_____
_____
_____

B. Synthesize. Use the chart in Organize above. Fill in the blanks of the advertisement with the correct information.

The Ultrasonic Bath: A Human _____ _____

Just Climb in and _____ a Button!

Cleans and _____ you in less than 15 minutes.

Uses _____ to Vibrate the _____ Right off of you!

Available Soon in Stores Near You!

09

Ghost Hunter

Guesswork

Discuss your answers to these questions with your classmates.

1. What can you see in these pictures? Do any of them look like real ghosts?
2. What would you do if you saw a ghost in real life?
3. How do you think people find ghosts?

▲ The West Coast Ghost and Paranormal Society is a Phoenix, Arizona based group of paranormal investigators. They seek to find ghosts. (left) Andy Rice, the lead investigator, is taking temperature readings in a haunted house; (middle) two members of the society are setting up a long-range IR camera; (right) ghost hunters are discussing camera angles at a command center.

RH1-09
MP3

Ghost Hunter

▲ Brown Lady Ghost photo. Originally taken in 1936 and published in the magazine 'Countrylife' in the same year.

Many people believe in ghosts. But how do you know if they are real? Go on a ghost-hunting tour and see one for yourself! Professional ghost hunters will take you to explore all sorts of haunted places. With their expertise and modern equipment, maybe you'll get lucky and find a real ghost.

Most hunters use weapons to kill their prey, but ghosts can't be killed. Luckily, ghost hunters don't need to kill ghosts. They are just trying to find them. Instead of weapons, they use specialized electronic tools. Since most ghosts are invisible, these tools allow ghost hunters to detect ghosts without actually seeing them.

Ghost hunters have many different ideas about how to find ghosts. One popular tool is a thermometer. Many ghost hunters think that a ghost is colder than the area around it. Think about that the next time you walk through a cold spot. You might be walking through a ghost.

Popular ghost-hunting tools

EMF meter
This tool measures changes in the electro-magnetic field — invisible energy that is all around us.

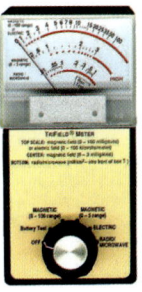

dowsing rod
The ghost hunter holds it and lets it "guide" him to the ghost.

thermometer
Ghost hunters use a special thermometer to find cold spots in the air.

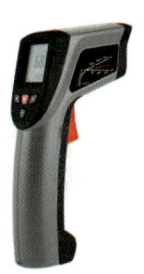

Some ghost-hunting tools are more common. Cameras of all kinds are used to capture pictures of ghosts. Often, things will show up in pictures that were never seen in person. Advanced ghost hunters have more tools than just a camera, but maybe a camera would be enough for you. So wait for a dark night, grab a camera, and go find some ghosts!

Vocabulary

A. Fill in each blank with the correct word from the word box.

explore	haunted	specialized	equipment
invisible	advanced	expert	

1. Dan is an _____ furniture maker. He has been a carpenter for 50 years.

2. I don't want to go into that old house. I heard that it is _____ .

3. I use a _____ car to carry my grandmother's wheelchair.

4. You are in a more _____ English class than I am, but I work harder than you.

5. Air is _____ , but when the wind blows you can feel it.

6. I love to _____ old caves and other strange places.

7. My mother just bought me new soccer _____ . I think it was really expensive.

B. Read the passage below. Match each phrase in red with its equivalent expression.

There are **various** jobs available for young people. The best way to get a job is to **appear** at the workplace and speak to the boss **personally**. This way the boss knows that you really care and will try hard at your new job.

1. in person _____

2. show up _____

3. all sorts of _____

Reading Comprehension

A. Main Ideas. Circle the answer that best completes each statement.

1. Ghost hunters use specialized tools to _____ .

   a. find and trap invisible ghosts
   b. find ghosts that cannot be seen

2. As a beginner ghost hunter, you'll probably _____ .

   a. try to find ghosts with simple ghost-hunting tools
   b. be able to find cold spots using specialized thermometers

B. Details. Write True or False after each statement.

1. Expert ghost hunters use advanced weapons to detect ghosts. _____

2. Ghost hunters think that ghosts lower the temperature of the air. _____

3. Ghosts may sometimes appear when you point a camera at them. _____

4. Ghost-hunters can take you on ghost-hunting tours. _____

C. Inferences. Based on your understanding of the text, choose the best way to complete each of these statements.

1. Ghost hunting equipment is probably _____ .

   a. expensive
   b. cheap

2. Most ghost hunters probably _____ .

   a. don't believe in ghosts
   b. think that ghosts are real

3. Ghost hunting tours probably _____ .

   a. find ghosts every time
   b. don't always find ghosts

A. Organize. Look at the list of facts regarding ghost hunting tools. Use the list of details to fill in the blanks.

- Detects the energy of ghosts.
- A ghost hunter holds it and lets it "guide" him to a ghost.
- A ghost is colder than the area around it.
- Invisible ghosts sometimes show up in photos.

Equipment	Purpose and Reasoning
thermometer	a. _____ b. Helps locate cold spots.
camera	a. _____ b. Takes pictures of ghosts.
EMF meter	a. _____ b. Electromagnetic energy is invisible energy that is all around us.
dowsing rod	a. _____

B. Synthesize. Use the chart in Organize above. Fill in the blanks in the Internet shopping website.

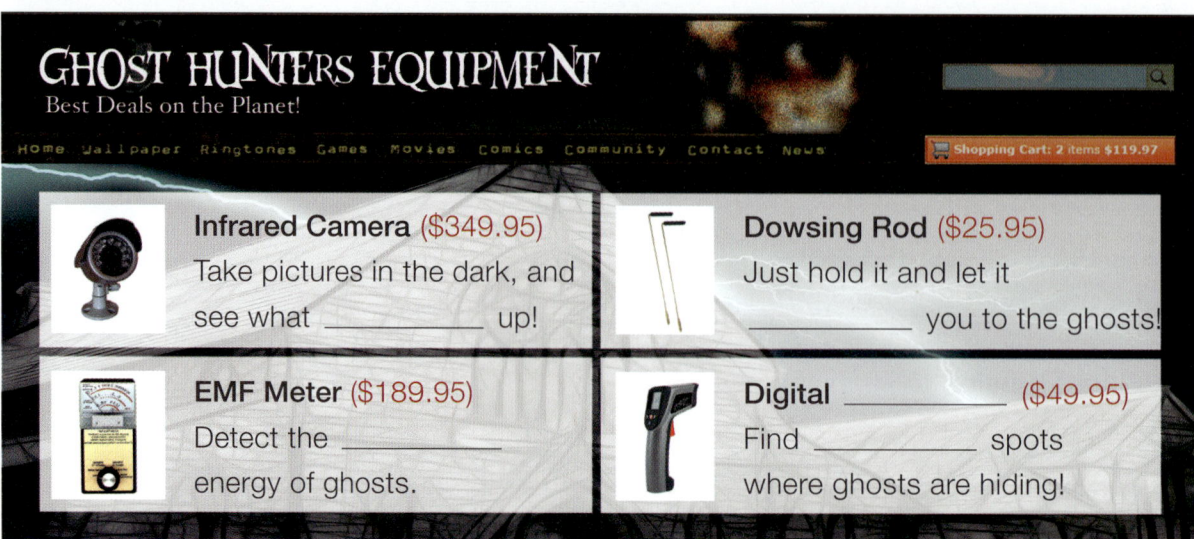

GHOST HUNTERS EQUIPMENT
Best Deals on the Planet!

Home Wallpaper Ringtones Games Movies Comics Community Contact News   Shopping Cart: 2 items $119.97

Infrared Camera ($349.95)
Take pictures in the dark, and see what _____ up!

Dowsing Rod ($25.95)
Just hold it and let it _____ you to the ghosts!

EMF Meter ($189.95)
Detect the _____ energy of ghosts.

Digital _____ ($49.95)
Find _____ spots where ghosts are hiding!

10

Did You See That?

Guesswork

Discuss your answers to these questions with your classmates.

1. What is this a picture of? Is it real?

2. What would you do if you saw this in the sky?

3. Do you think this thing might be dangerous?

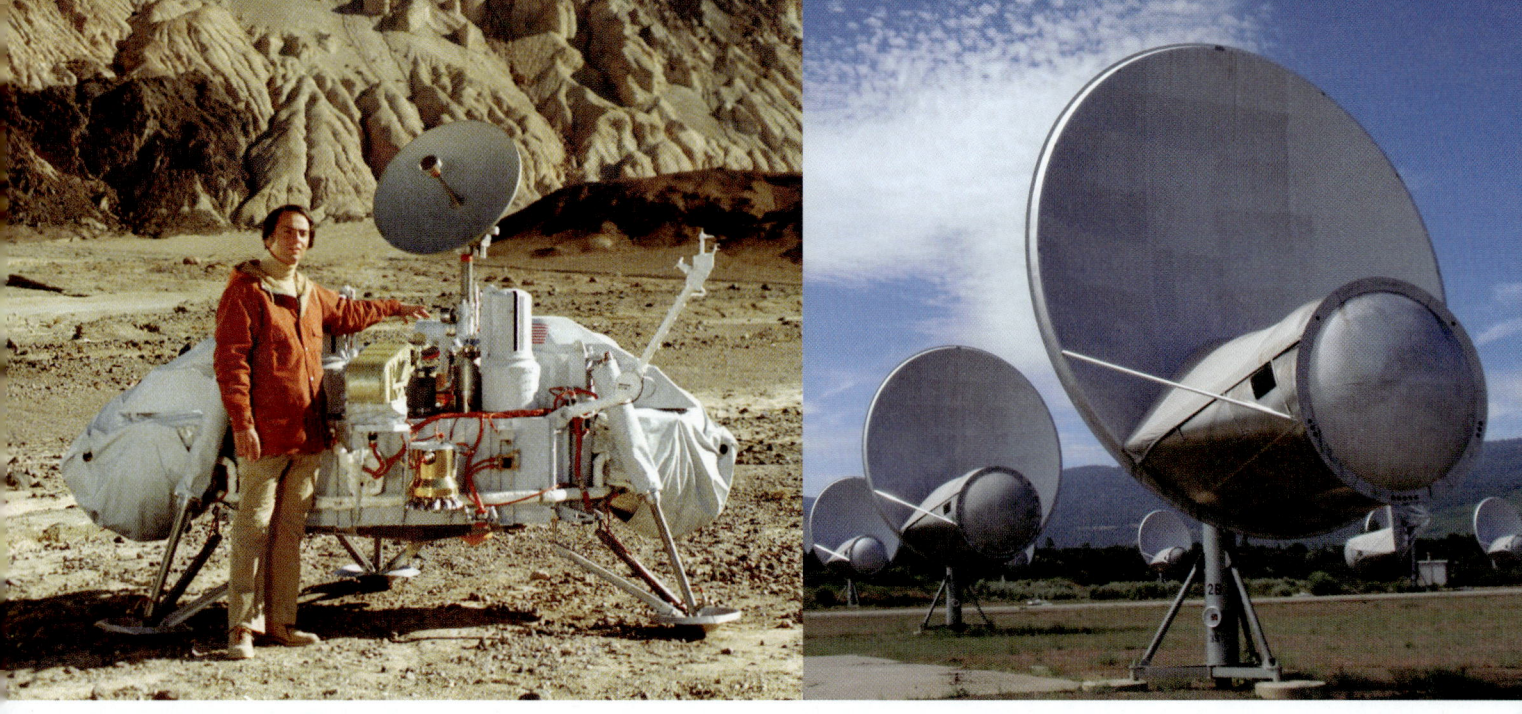

▲ Carl Sagan, a well-respected scientist in the field of outer space, investigated numerous reports of UFOs.

▲ The Allen Telescope Array (ATA) is a radio telescope specifically designed to seek out and communicate with alien life.

▲ Photo of one of the Triangle-UFOs which were seen over Belgium in the 1990s. From 1989 to 1991, around 3,500 UFO sightings were reported in Belgium.

RH1-10
MP3

Did You See That?

Zoology is the study of animals. Mythology is the study of myths. But what about ufology? It's the study of UFOs, of course.

UFO stands for Unidentified Flying Object. If somebody sees something in the sky, but nobody knows what it is, then it is a UFO. UFOs can be anything. Some are bright lights that move strangely. Others are big metal saucers, or small shiny spheres. Many people report touching, or even going inside UFOs.

THE UNKNOWN

This plaque commemorates the landmark of the mysterious disappearance of FREDERICK VALENTICH on 21 October 1978.

Frederick was flying a Cessna 182L, and at this point he changed direction to south from the lighthouse towards the sea.

Twelve minutes flying south from here at precisely 19:12:28 hrs radio transmission was cut off and in his last radio contact he explained "that strange aircraft is hovering on top of me again, and it is not an aircraft......."

After an extensive land and sea search, no trace was ever found of the Cessna VH-DSJ or of FREDERICK VALENTICH.

And so to this day, his disappearance remains a mystery.

▲ On 21 October 1978, 21-year-old pilot Frederick Valentich went missing over Bass Strait. Some claim he was abducted by a UFO while others concluded it was simply a hoax designed by Valentich in order to obtain life insurance money.

Years ago, the US government became concerned about increasing reports of UFOs. They thought that these strange flying objects might be dangerous, but they weren't sure if UFOs were real or not. So they started an organization that investigated UFO sightings across the country. It was the beginning of ufology.

Ufology is a difficult field of study. Often, the only evidence of a UFO sighting is the story of the person who saw it. A person can lie about what they saw, or they could just be confused. It is a *ufologist's job to separate fact from fiction.

The government doesn't support ufology research anymore. There just wasn't enough proof that UFOs are real. Ufology isn't dead, though. There are new reports of UFOs every day. Ufologists have a lot of work to do.

*ufologist a person who studies UFOs

Vocabulary

A. Circle the correct answer and write it in the blank.

1. Spheres are _____ .
    a. square   **b.** round

2. A report is someone's _____ .
    a. lie   **b.** story

3. To be concerned is to _____ .
    a. worry   **b.** forget

4. A sighting of something is the act of _____ it.
    a. seeing   **b.** touching

5. To separate is to _____ .
    a. take apart   **b.** put together

6. An organization is a group of _____ .
    a. UFOs   **b.** people

7. Fiction is a story that is _____ .
    a. true   **b.** false

8. To support is to _____ .
    a. help   **b.** hurt

9. Evidence is the same as _____ .
    a. fiction   **b.** facts

10. Zoologists work with _____ .
    a. plants   **b.** animals

B. Draw lines to make correct sentences. Write the completed sentences below.

1. I'd like to build a car •   • across the country •   • I can do it.

2. Betty traveled •   • but I'm not sure if •   • where he is.

3. Sam is missing •   • and nobody knows •   • in an old van.

(1) I'd like to build a car _____

(2) Betty traveled _____

(3) Sam is missing _____

Reading Comprehension

A. Main Ideas. Circle the answer that best completes each statement.

1. The study of UFOs is called _____ .

   a. ufology   **b.** ufologist

2. A UFO is anything in the sky that is _____ .

   a. unidentified   **b.** flying

3. The US government started studying ufology because _____ .

   a. they thought UFOs might be dangerous
   b. they were concerned about UFO organizations

B. Details. Circle the answers that best complete each statement.

1. If you see a(n) (1) _____ in the sky, you might have seen a (2) _____ .

(1) **a.** bright light   **b.** airplane   **c.** cloud

(2) **a.** ufologist   **b.** ufology   **c.** UFO

2. Some people might (1) _____ about seeing UFOs, so ufologists need to (2) _____ .

(1) **a.** cry   **b.** lie   **c.** die

(2) **a.** find the truth   **b.** confuse their story   **c.** believe their stories

C. Inferences. Read each statement and decide if you think it is likely or unlikely. Check the appropriate box.

	Likely	Unlikely
1. Ufologists believe every UFO story they hear.	☐	☐
2. Some people might think that strange-looking planes are UFOs.	☐	☐
3. The government isn't worried about UFOs anymore.	☐	☐
4. Most ufologists have been inside a UFO.	☐	☐

A. Organize. Arrange the facts about the origins of ufology into the correct sequence.

1	Many people report seeing strange things in the sky.
	Government stops supporting ufology, but ufology remains popular.
	The government becomes concerned that UFOs are dangerous.
	The US government hears about increasing reports of UFOs.
	The government starts an organization that investigates reports of UFOs.

B. Synthesize. Use the chart in Organize above. Fill in the blanks of the advertisement with the correct information.

Ufology—a New Science!

Early this summer the government started a new organization to **i**_____ an increasing number of UFO **s**_____. A government official said that the government is "**c**_____ that UFOs may be **d**_____." No one knows how long the government will **s**_____ this new organization.

City of Ghosts

Guesswork

Discuss your answers to these questions with your classmates.

1. Imagine you are walking through here at night. Would you feel scared?

2. What kinds of things might you see?

3. Do you think this is a safe place?

City of Ghosts

▲ **Bhangarh** is so haunted that the government won't build a historical office in the ruins — a requirement for all historical sites in India.

Rajasthan

RH1-11
MP3

You've probably heard of haunted houses. But how about a haunted city? Bhangarh is an abandoned town in Rajasthan, India. People say that it is one of the most haunted places in the world. Even the government believes so. They forbid anyone from entering Bhangarh between sunset and sunrise, the time when ghosts are most likely to appear!

Bhangarh is renowned for its beautiful ruins and temples. But there is a darker side to the ruined city. The story begins with a wicked magician and a beautiful princess. The magician fell in love with the princess, but he could not marry her. He made an evil potion that would

▲ There are no roofs on any of the buildings left in Bhangarh. Locals say that whenever a house is built in the area, its roof collapses!

▲ **The signboard warns**: "Entering the borders of Bhangarh before sunrise and after sunset is strictly prohibited."

make the princess come to him. Then, he put the potion in her room.

Luckily, the princess was clever. She threw the potion onto a big rock. The rock rolled away, right onto the magician, and crushed him. As he was dying, the magician cursed the entire city. Shortly afterwards, the city was struck by famine and then abandoned. Now local people tell stories of strange things, like music coming from the empty ruins, and photographs of the city with strange colors in them.

Like most ghost stories, you might have to see Bhangarh yourself to believe it. Just be careful when you visit. You don't want to be caught there after dark.

Did You Know?

Another legend claims that Bhangarh was cursed by a guru named Balu Nath. The guru gave the king permission to build Bhangarh, but when the buildings grew too high, the guru cursed the city because the buildings' shadows touched his desert home.

Vocabulary

A. Answer the questions in complete sentences. The first one has been done for you.

1. The town is abandoned now. Is it full or empty?

It is empty.

2. The picture was created by a renowned painter. Is he famous or unknown?

_____

3. Sunrise is at 5 a.m. Does the sun go up at 5 or go down at 5?

_____

4. A wicked man lives in the house next to mine. Is the man good or evil?

_____

5. The witch made a potion to cure my disease. Should I eat it or drink it?

_____

6. The people of Africa are often struck by famine. Are they often thirsty or hungry?

_____

B. Choose the answer closest in meaning to the underlined part of the sentence.

1. I lost my wallet, but shortly afterwards a man returned it to me.

   a. not much later   **b.** after a while

2. Get out of mom's closet. You don't want to be caught there when she comes home!

   a. be stuck   **b.** be found

3. They will most likely be able to pass the exam.

   a. almost   **b.** probably

Reading Comprehension

A. Main Ideas. Complete the statement by circling the correct choice for each blank.

The passage is mainly about the **1.** _____ of **2.** _____ . So the main idea is that **3.** _____ .

1. a. legend   b. ghosts

2. a. an abandoned city   b. a ruined temple

3. a. the people of Bhangarh abandoned the city to ghosts
    b. the legend says a wicked magician cursed the city of Bhangarh

B. Details. Write True or False after each statement.

1. The ruins of Bhangarh are known for their beauty.   _____

2. The magician tried to trick the beautiful princess.   _____

3. The princess was clever so she threw the potion at the magician.   _____

4. After the magician died, his ghost cursed the city.   _____

5. Local people hear music in the abandoned ruins of Bhangarh.   _____

6. The government forbids anyone from entering Bhangarh before   _____
sunset and after sunrise.

C. Inferences. Decide which of the statements can be inferred from the passage. Check the correct answers. (Choose two.)

_____ **1.** People visit Bhangarh to see if it is really haunted.

_____ **2.** Bhangarh is the most popular tourist spot in India.

_____ **3.** Tourists have been killed at Bhangarh after dark.

_____ **4.** Bhangarh has been abandoned for a long time.

A. Organize. Write each statement in the correct box.

- An abandoned city in India that is said to be haunted
- Local people claim to hear music in the ruins.
- Rajasthan, India
- Legend says that a wicked magician cursed the city.

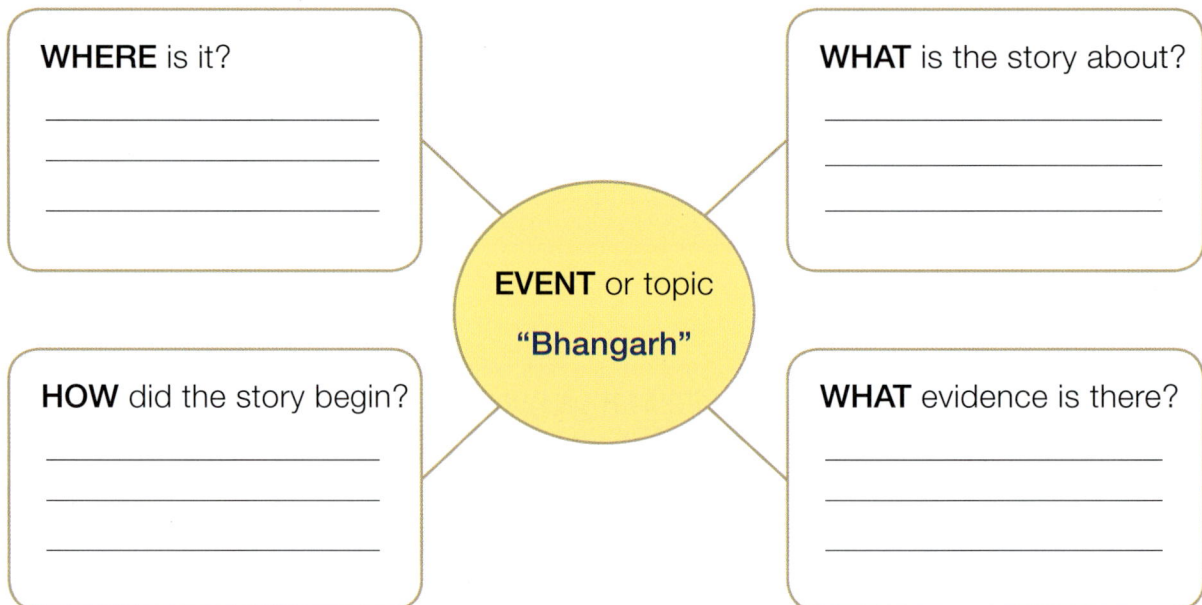

WHERE is it?

_____
_____
_____

WHAT is the story about?

_____
_____
_____

EVENT or topic

"Bhangarh"

HOW did the story begin?

_____
_____
_____

WHAT evidence is there?

_____
_____
_____

B. Synthesize. Use the chart in Organize above. Fill in the blanks of the advertisement with the correct information.

Bhangarh: India's Haunted City

Located in beautiful Rajasthan, India, the **a**_____ city of Bhangarh is known for its beautiful **r**_____ and dark past.

Legend says that a **w**_____ magician **c**_____ the city.

Locals will tell you of strange events, such as **m**_____ coming mysteriously from the ruins.

Come and see if the stories are true!

12
U N I T

Living in a Maze

Guesswork

Discuss your answers to these questions with your classmates.

1. What words would you use to describe this place? How does it make you feel?

2. Does this seem like a nice place to live?

3. Why do you think people live here?

▲ **An aerial view of Kowloon Walled City in 1989** In 1987, 33,000 people lived in Kowloon Walled City — in the space of only 0.01 square miles.

▲ An outer edge of the Walled City in 1991

▲ Most of the alleyways were only 1-2 meters wide. Motorcycles could fit, but not cars.

RH1-12
MP3

Living in a Maze

Can you imagine living in a giant maze? Some people didn't have to imagine. They actually lived in one. It was called Kowloon Walled City. The buildings were connected by so many passageways that you could walk across the city without ever touching the ground.

Kowloon Walled City was located in Hong Kong, China. The British ruled Hong Kong for many years, but the Walled City had no government. Neither Britain nor China took responsibility for it. Over time, the city grew on its own and became lawless. Without rules, people added onto the city however they wanted. Residents made stairs and passageways that went from rooftop to rooftop and window to window. These "roads" were so dense that the lower alleys got almost no sunlight. The residents had to install electric lights just so they could see during the day.

Many kinds of criminals hid inside the city. Hong Kong police officers wouldn't even go inside alone. They thought it was too dangerous. For this reason, the Hong Kong government decided to demolish the city. It took them six years to remove all of the people.

After the city was torn down, a park was built in its place. Only a few ruins of Kowloon Walled City remain today.

Did You Know?
Even though many criminals made their home in Kowloon Walled City, it was a safe place for families as well. The families took care of one another, and made sure that children were looked after.

▲ 1898   ▲ 1989   ▲ 2009

Vocabulary

A. Circle the answer that fits best with the word in red.

1. maze   complicated / simple / strange

2. rule   control / listen / obey

3. passageway on / off / through

4. criminal   punish / accept / reward

5. demolish   create / destroy / build

6. remove   take away / move towards / go into

7. remain   leave / stay / believe

8. decide   lose / make / choose

9. dense   tall / short / heavy

10. connect   together / over / within

B. Fill in the blanks using the expressions from the box.

tear down	take responsibility for	for this reason

1. Bill, did you break that lamp? You should _____ your actions.

2. You never do your homework. _____ I am moving you to a lower class.

3. They're going to _____ that old skyscraper. Let's go watch!

74

Reading Comprehension

A. Main Ideas. Circle the correct answer for each question.

1. Which word best describes Kowloon Walled City?

    a. responsible

    b. lawless

2. How was the Walled City like a maze?

    a. It was designed to trap people.

    b. There were many ways to move through it.

3. Why was the Walled City destroyed?

    a. it was too dangerous

    b. it was too dark

B. Details. Write Opinion or Fact after each statement.

1. China should have taken responsibility for the Walled City.   _____

2. The passageways of the Walled City blocked the sun.   _____

3. Pieces of the Walled City still survive.   _____

4. The Walled City was a horrible place to live.   _____

C. Inferences. Decide which of the statements can be inferred from the passage. Check the correct answers. (Choose two.)

_____ **1.** Hong Kong police officers never entered the Walled City.

_____ **2.** Residents of the Walled City changed their apartments as they liked.

_____ **3.** Many people didn't want to leave the Walled City.

_____ **4.** The residents of the Walled City paid for the park to be built.

Writing

A. Organize. Look at the outline of the main ideas in the passage. Fill in the details that illustrate these main ideas. Choose from the list of details.

- Passageways connected all of the buildings.
- Police officers would not enter the city alone.
- Criminals hid inside the city.
- The lower alleys were so dark that electric lights were installed.

OUTLINE	
Main Ideas	**Details**
1. Residents added onto the city however they wanted.	a. _____ b. _____ _____
2. The Hong Kong government thought the city was dangerous.	a. The city was demolished. b. _____ c. _____

B. Synthesize. Use the chart in Organize above. Complete the conversation between a former resident of Kowloon Walled City and a reporter.

Reporter: What was it like, living in such a crowded place?

Resident: It was dangerous because _____ hid inside the city, but most

people were helpful. We built many _____ so that we could

_____ easily from point to point.

Reporter: Wasn't that dangerous?

Resident: Maybe. The lower _____ were so dark that we installed

_____ _____!

13
U N I T

To Be an Astronaut

Guesswork

Discuss your answers to these questions with your classmates.

1. What is the kid doing in the machine? Does it look like fun?

2. Where do you think the kid is?

3. Does this look like an interesting place?

To Be an Astronaut

RH1-13
MP3

Can you imagine what it's like to be an astronaut? To feel like you weigh nothing? To control a giant space shuttle? Well, you don't just have to imagine. You can experience it yourself!

At the United States Space Camp, in Huntsville, Alabama, boys and girls from around the world train just like real astronauts. For six days they wear astronaut suits, eat astronaut food, and learn all about space. They even get to experience weightlessness with a special machine. It's called the Space Shot simulator.

Campers can choose what they focus on. Some campers learn how to build and control robots. Others learn all about flying airplanes and even spend time in jet simulators. Many campers choose to do Mars Training, a special course designed to teach a camper everything about space travel. These courses are fun and exciting, but they are serious too. Each course helps prepare the campers for their final challenge — a simulated space shuttle flight.

▲ From top: rockets in the rocket park at Huntsville space camp; Space Shot Simulator; jet simulator

▲ Space flight deck

▲ Mission control

Everybody works together for this last activity. Campers can choose to stay on the ground and help guide the space shuttle, or they can decide to be astronauts and sit at the controls of the simulator. Each camper has a unique and important job. This may be the most important lesson of space camp. Without teamwork, astronauts could never survive in space.

▲ Space shuttle

A. Answer the questions in complete sentences. The first one has been done for you.

1. Henry weighs a lot. Is he tall or heavy?

He is heavy.

2. I want to train to be a firefighter. Do I want to teach or practice?

_____

3. A fireman's suit is made of fabric that doesn't melt. Are his clothes special or normal?

_____

4. The machine helps us simulate a real explosion. Does it make a real or a fake explosion?

_____

5. Lisa teaches students how to build robots. Do the students learn how to make or use robots?

_____

6. Becca thinks that her homework is challenging. Is it difficult or easy?

_____

B. Fill in the blanks using the expressions from the box.

at the controls of	designed to	focus on

1. School was so much fun today! I got to sit _____ a real plane!

2. Today we're going to _____ pilots and how they fly.

3. This plane is very special. It is _____ go faster than sound!

Reading Comprehension

A. Main Ideas. Circle the correct answer to the question.

1. What is the main idea of this passage?

    a. Campers can choose which course they want to focus on.
    b. The Space Shot simulator is the biggest challenge of space camp.
    c. Space Camp teaches campers how to build robots just like astronauts.
    d. Space Camp gives campers the experience of training like a real astronaut.

B. Details. Circle the answer that best completes each statement.

1. Campers get to _____ .

    a. fly in a space shuttle   **b.** feel like they weigh nothing

2. Every camper _____ for the final challenge.

    a. works together   **b.** does Mars Training

3. Some campers choose to take _____ in flying airplanes.

    a. a course   **b.** a challenge

4. The space shuttle simulation teaches campers about the importance of _____ .

    a. Mars training   **b.** teamwork

C. Inferences. Read each statement and decide if you think it is likely or unlikely. Check the appropriate box.

	Likely	Unlikely
1. Real astronauts use the Space Shot simulator.	☐	☐
2. Campers are ready to travel in space after they finish Space Camp.	☐	☐
3. Campers get to eat food in space, just like real astronauts.	☐	☐
4. Students get to learn how a space shuttle works.	☐	☐

Writing

A. **Organize.** Look at the table of space camp activities. Use the list of details to fill in the blanks.

- Provides the experience of flying in a plane.
- Teaches the camper about traveling in space.
- Each camper has a unique and important job.
- Gives the experience of weightlessness.

Activity	Description and Purpose
Space shuttle flight simulator	a. _____ b. Teaches the importance of teamwork.
Mars training	a. _____
Space Shot	a. _____
Jet simulator	a. _____

B. **Synthesize.** Use the chart in Organize above. Fill in the blanks in the advertisement for Space Camp.

Want to travel in space? Come to Space Camp and train just like a real astronaut!

Mars Training: A fantastic look at space travel. Campers will learn all about _____ _____ _____ .

Space Shot: A special machine that gives the campers the experience of _____ .

Jet Simulator: A machine that simulates the experience of _____ in a _____ .

Space Shuttle Flight Simulator: The final challenge of space camp. Each student works together to learn the importance of _____ .

14

U N I T

Life in Space

Guesswork

Discuss your answers to these questions with your classmates.

1. Describe the picture. How do you think the astronaut feels?

2. Does space seem like a place that humans can live?

3. What problems will the astronaut have, being so far away from Earth?

▲ **International Space Station (ISS)** 14 different nations have launched spacecraft from all over the world to help build and maintain the ISS. It is the the most expensive object ever made.

RH1-14
MP3

Life in Space

People have homes everywhere: at the tops of mountains, in the middle of the ocean, and deep under the earth. Some people even dream of living on other planets. And we're a lot closer than you think!

Since October 2000, people from 15 different nations have lived in space on board the International Space Station (ISS). Astronauts staying in the ISS conduct experiments and take care of the space station. Maintaining the ISS may be one of the most important

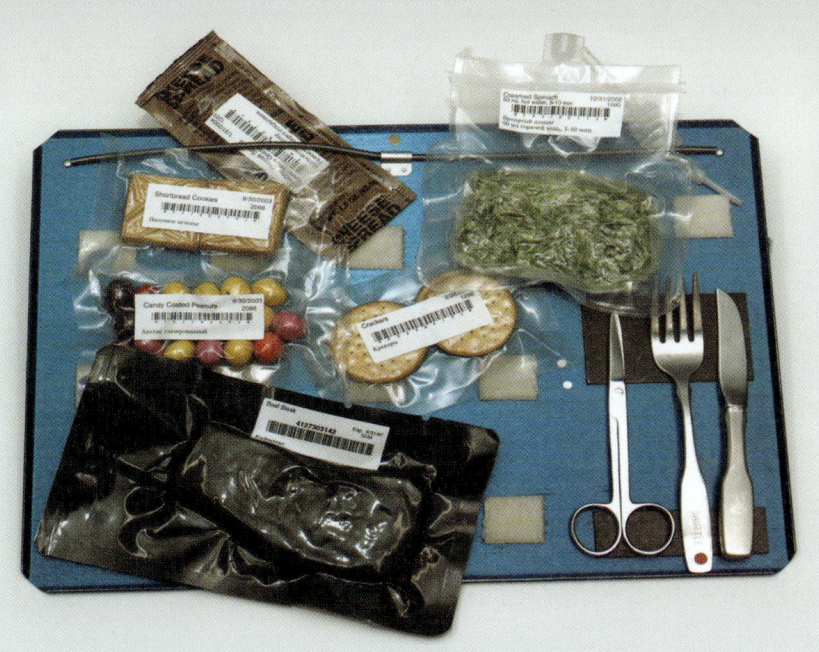

▲ Space Food; Each trip on the ISS lasts about 3 months and requires about 2,700 kg of food.

▲ Sometimes there is not enough space to sleep in the ISS, but it's not a big problem. Because they are weightless, the scientists just attach their sleeping bags to the wall!

experiments of all. Through the ISS, scientists hope to learn more about long-term space travel.

Many things that are simple on Earth are difficult in space. The human body changes after being weightless for a long time. Scientists have to exercise on a special machine to keep their muscles strong. Using the bathroom also becomes complicated when gravity isn't there to help you.

On the ISS, food, oxygen and water are all limited. Each time they visit the station, astronauts must bring enough food for their entire trip. Special machines clean the air and make it breathable. To save water, scientists use sponges to clean themselves. They even use edible toothpaste to clean their teeth, so they don't need to rinse.

Despite these difficulties, we have become skilled at surviving in space. Next thing you know, we'll have homes on Mars!

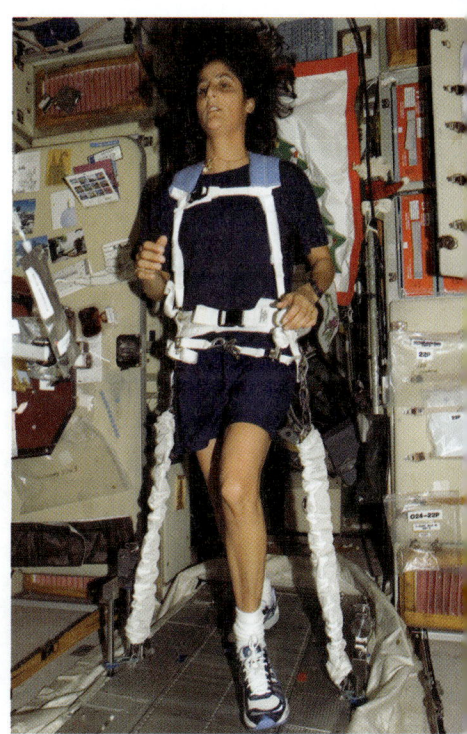

▲ An astronaut is attached to the TVIS treadmill with bungee cords aboard the International Space Station.

Vocabulary

A. Circle the best answer.

1. NYC just built a new fire **experiment / station** in Queens.

2. I can't **maintain / limit** good grades in Spanish. It is too difficult.

3. This puzzle is too **complicated / breathable** for children.

4. Did you know that they make **edible / long-term** paper? It tastes like oranges.

5. In science class, we did a fun **gravity / experiment**. We blew up a watermelon!

6. This cake needs a(n) **entire / simple** stick of butter. It's going to be delicious!

B. Write each word in the correct column.

| juggling | an airplane | a boat | a tree | |
| a mountain | a video game | a sport | a train | a tower |

1. at the top of

_____

_____

_____

2. on board

_____

_____

_____

3. become skilled at

_____

_____

_____

Reading Comprehension

A. Main Ideas. Circle the answer that best completes each statement.

1. The passage is mainly about _____ .

   a. living on other planets   **b.** living in space

2. Life in space is more _____ than life on earth.

   a. complicated   **b.** simple

3. The ISS may teach scientists how to _____ .

   a. survive on other planets   **b.** become weightless on Earth

B. Details. Circle the answers that best complete each statement.

1. Scientists must (1)_____ on the space station, or their (2)_____ will weaken.

(1) **a.** experiment   **b.** stay   **c.** exercise

(2) **a.** gravity   **b.** muscles   **c.** science

2. Because (1)_____ is limited, scientists use (2)_____ to make the air breathable.

(1) **a.** food   **b.** water   **c.** oxygen

(2) **a.** special machines   **b.** sponges   **c.** edible toothpaste

C. Inferences. Decide which of the statements can be inferred from the passage. Check the correct answers. (Choose two.)

_____ **1.** Scientists rarely brush their teeth on the space station.

_____ **2.** Using the bathroom is difficult in space.

_____ **3.** Astronauts can stay in space for many years at a time.

_____ **4.** The ISS has many complicated parts.

Writing

A. Organize. Look at the photo. Fill in the blanks.

WHO is the subject of the photo?

A_____ on the ISS.

WHAT are the astronauts doing?

They are **e**_____ a meal on the ISS.

HOW do you know the astronauts are in space?

They are **w**_____ .

WHERE did the food come from?

The astronauts **b**_____ it with them.

B. Synthesize. Use the picture and questions in Organize above. Complete the letter from an astronaut to his wife.

Dear Liz,

Can you believe it? I've been in space for one whole month! _____
(What's his job?-3words)

has been strange and exciting. I am very busy doing experiments, but my work is not

the strange part. Eating meals is actually the weirdest part of _____ .
(Where is he staying?-4words)

Because _____ , the food floats around. If we spill a drink, it doesn't
(Why does the food float around?-3words)

fall to the floor. Instead, it forms a bubble and floats away! Anyway, I need to get back

to work now. I miss you dearly, and can't wait to see you again.

Love,

Ryan

15
UNIT

Making Music

Guesswork

Discuss your answers to these questions with your classmates.

1. What are the men doing?

2. How could they entertain themselves?

3. Can you imagine how the bow might provide entertainment?

RH1-15
MP3

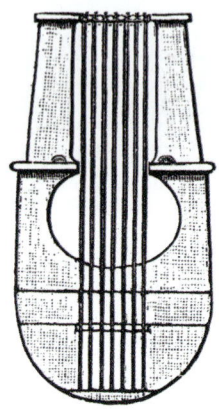

▲ The *cithara* was an early stringed instrument in Greece. It is composed of a box with strings coming out of the top.

Making Music

Peple use music to express their feelings. We dance to it when we're happy. We sing and play it when we're sad or angry. Sometimes we make it just because we want to!

Music takes many forms, but one thing is common to most music of today: the guitar. Turn on the radio, and there's a good chance you'll hear one. Guitars are everywhere, but do you know where they come from?

Imagine an ancient human hunting in the forest. He picks up his bow, pulls the bowstring back and releases it. It snaps forward and makes a pleasant twang, just like a one-stringed guitar. Could this ancient hunter's bow have been one of the first stringed instruments?

The bow harp is the first stringed instrument to show up in ancient art. Made in Egypt, the bow harp was shaped like a hunting bow, but instead of one string it had many. Soon other stringed instruments were made, except these had a large box at the bottom. The box made the sound larger and fuller. Eventually these instruments evolved into the modern guitar.

Now we've gone even further. Some guitars don't even have the box to make the sound bigger anymore. Electric guitars use speakers to make their sound big. And to think it all started with an ancient hunter and his bow.

▲ Musician holding a cithara in her left and tuning a small harp with the right: Part of a Roman fresco from Pompeii in the National Archaeological Museum of Naples, Italy

▲ An ancient Egyptian harp on display in the British Museum

Vocabulary

A. Answer the questions in complete sentences. The first one has been done for you.

1. The policeman released the dog and it ran away. Did he let go of it or hold onto it?

He let go of it.

2. When our food eventually came, it was cold. Did the food come quickly or slowly?

_____

3. The man used his bow to hunt the zebra. Was he shooting or trapping the zebra?

_____

4. That book is ancient. Don't touch it. Is it old or new?

_____

5. I snapped the rubber band at his arm. Did the rubber band move quickly or slowly?

_____

6. The weather is very pleasant today. Is the weather nice or bad?

_____

B. Choose the answer closest in meaning to the underlined part of the sentence.

1. There's a good chance that your wallet is in my car. I'll check when I get home.

    a. It's likely   **b.** I know

2. You shouldn't show up at a party when nobody invited you.

    a. appear   **b.** dance

3. Pull this branch back and I will cut it.

    a. Move away   **b.** Move forward

Reading Comprehension

A. Main Ideas. Circle the answer that best completes each statement.

1. The first stringed instrument could have been made from a _____.

    a. hunter's bow   **b.** guitar

2. The guitar evolved from stringed instruments _____.

    a. like the bow harp   **b.** with a box on the bottom

3. Electric guitars use _____ to help them sound louder.

    a. strings   **b.** speakers

B. Details. Circle the correct answer for each question.

1. A hunting bow is like a guitar because _____.

    a. it is very popular across the world
    b. it is built to make music
    c. it can make a pleasant sound

2. Why was a box added to stringed instruments?

    a. To help it evolve into the guitar.
    b. To make it easier to hold.
    c. To make it easier to hear.

C. Inferences. Read each statement and decide if you think it is likely or unlikely. Check the appropriate box.

	Likely	Unlikely
1. The bow harp is not very common today.	☐	☐
2. Ancient hunters made the first guitars.	☐	☐
3. Without speakers, electric guitars are hard to hear.	☐	☐
4. Ancient bow harps were used to hunt animals.	☐	☐

Writing

A. Organize. Write each answer (a-f) in the correct place in the chart.

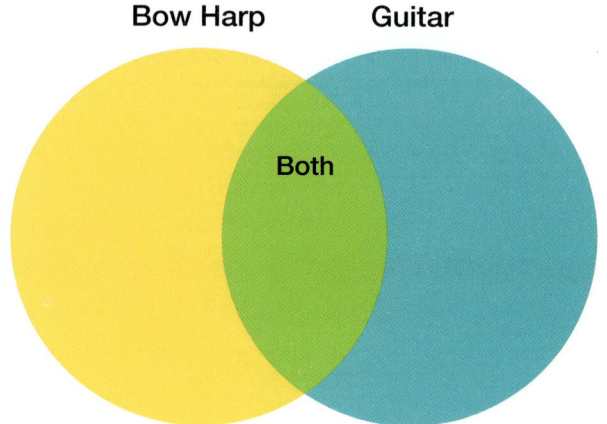

Bow Harp   **Guitar**

Both

a. strings can be pulled back and
   released to make sound
b. has a box to make sound larger
c. shaped like a hunting bow
d. has many strings
e. popular across the world
f. comes from Egypt

B. Synthesize. Read Organize above and write each word from the word bank in
the correct box below.

| guitar strings | popular | bow-shape |
| box | from Egypt | many strings(x2) |

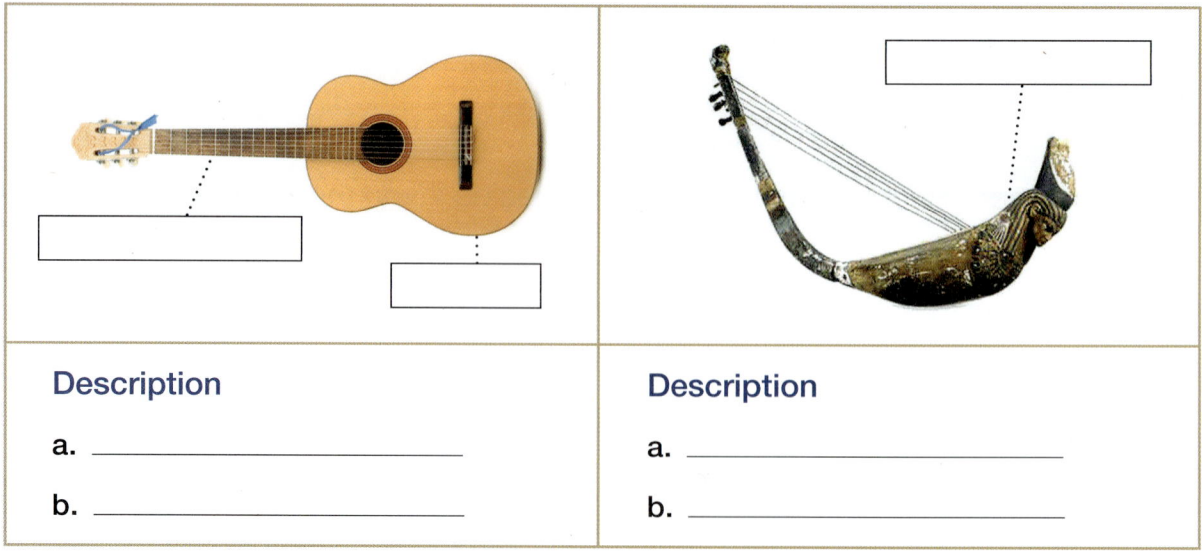

Description

a. _____

b. _____

Description

a. _____

b. _____

16

Playing with Food

Guesswork

Discuss your answers to these questions with your classmates.

1. Describe the picture. What colors and shapes do you see?

2. Which food in the picture is your favorite to eat?

3. Can you think of any uses for these fruits and vegetables besides as food?

▲ The Vegetable Orchestra formed in Vienna, Austria in 1998, and they now play concerts all over the world.

▲ **From top:** cucumber recorder, pumpkin drum, carrot trumpet

Playing with Food

Have you ever played the piano or the violin? How about a vegetable? It may sound strange, but the Vienna Vegetable Orchestra plays music with only vegetables.

The orchestra has eleven members. Each performer is interested in different kinds of music and art. They work together to create new, and sometimes strange, music. Their goal is to make music which the audience can hear, see, touch, smell, and taste.

The instruments are bought and made just hours before each performance. Only fresh vegetables are used. The

The Vegetable Orchestra also uses certain kitchen tools, like knives and mixers, as additional instruments during their performances.

performers use drills and knives to transform these vegetables into all sorts of creative instruments. There are cucumber recorders, pumpkin drums, and even carrot trumpets. When the concert is finished, all of the vegetables are cooked into a soup. Then the soup is eaten by the performers and the audience.

They do not play Mozart, or Beethoven, and they definitely don't play Michael Jackson. They don't even know what their music will sound like until they make the instruments. Their music is improvised and changes every concert. This means that every show is unique. There are new instruments and new music for each one. And of course a new meal to share with the audience at the end of every performance.

The Vegetable Orchestra would be hard to hear if they didn't use modern technology. Sensitive microphones are used to pick up every little sound that the vegetables make.

Vocabulary

▲ Gansterer Troyer is playing with a carrot trumpet at a concert.

A. Circle the correct answer and write it in the blank.

1. An audience _____ .

    a. watches a performance

    b. creates a performance

2. Members of a group are people that _____ .

    a. work together   **b.** work apart

3. An instrument can be used to _____ .

    a. make music   **b.** listen to music

4. To transform something is to _____ .

    a. sell it   **b.** change it

5. A drill is a kind of _____ .

    a. instrument   **b.** tool

B. Draw lines to make correct sentences. Write the completed sentences below.

1. Have you ever   •   • that new piano   •   • with your toes?

2. Do you know what •   • played the piano   •   • when he is finished playing?

3. Should we   •   • stand up and clap •   • sounds like?

    (1) Have you ever _____

    (2) Do you know what _____

    (3) Should we _____

Reading Comprehension

A. **Main Ideas.** Complete the statement by circling the correct choice for each blank.

The passage is mainly about the **1.** _____ of **2.** _____ . So the main idea is that **3.** _____ .

1. **a.** creativity   **b.** success

2. **a.** a unique audience   **b.** a special group of performers

3. **a.** the success of the Vegetable Orchestra is thanks to their unique audiences
     b. the Vegetable Orchestra creates unique music for audiences around the world

B. **Details.** Write True or False after each statement.

1. The members of the vegetable orchestra have similar tastes. _____

2. The music of the vegetable orchestra is made for all five senses. _____

3. The performers use the same instruments each time. _____

4. The audience eats the instruments after the performance. _____

5. The performers eat their instruments during the show. _____

6. The music is different for each performance. _____

C. **Inferences.** Decide which of the statements can be inferred from the passage. Check the correct answers. (Choose one.)

_____ **1.** Carrots are the most popular instrument of the vegetable orchestra.

_____ **2.** The vegetable orchestra often performs popular music.

_____ **3.** The vegetable orchestra uses strawberries to make music.

_____ **4.** Some instruments are played by mouth and others by hand.

Writing

A. Organize. Look at the outline of the main ideas in the passage. Use the list of details to fill in the blanks.

- Music is improvised.
- Instruments are made of vegetables.
- After the show, the audience and performers eat the instruments.
- Instruments are made just hours before the performance.

OUTLINE	
Main Ideas	**Details**
1. The Vegetable Orchestra gives a strange performance.	a. _____ b. _____ _____
2. Each performance is unique.	a. _____ b. _____ _____

B. Synthesize. Use the chart in Organize above. Fill in the blanks of the advertisement with the correct information.

Music with Vegetables!

When: April 22nd

Where: The Portsmouth Brewery

Come watch the Vienna Vegetable Orchestra perform with **i**_____ made of **v**_____ .
Each performance is **u**_____ .
The music is **i**_____ , and the instruments are made just hours before the **p**_____ .

Guesswork

Discuss your answers to these questions with your classmates.

1. Which picture is scarier? Why?

2. Compare the pictures. How are the two men different? alike?

3. What would you do if you met either of these men?

▲ German stories claim that Vlad the Impaler killed at least 80,000 people. They also say he burned whole villages to the ground, and impaled, tortured, burned, skinned, roasted, and boiled his enemies.

RH1-17
MP3

A Terrible Monster

Dracula is a frightening monster that may haunt your dreams. He uses two sharp teeth to bite your neck and suck out your blood. If you don't die, then you'll change into a monster just like Dracula: a vampire. Vampires can transform into anything: dogs, bats, rats, and even fog. They can squeeze through the smallest cracks, and are stronger than 20 men. Of all vampires, Dracula is the most fearsome. But did you know that Dracula was a real person, as well as a fictional monster?

The original monster was created by Bram Stoker, for his book, Dracula. Stoker was inspired by a real person; a terrible ruler named Vlad the Impaler. At least, that was Vlad's nickname. His real last name was Dracula.

Vlad was nicknamed "the Impaler" because of how he killed his enemies. Many stories describe his unique and painful form of execution. He would drive long sharpened stakes into the ground, and then impale his victims. It was a slow and horrible death. Vlad would leave the dead bodies hanging for days. This gruesome sight reminded others to follow his rules.

Some stories even claim that Vlad the Impaler drank the blood of his victims, after it ran down the sharpened stakes. Even if this were true, Vlad wasn't a real vampire. To his victims, however, he must have seemed like one terrible monster.

▲ Bram Stoker

▲ Woodblock print of Vlad the Impaler dining in the presence of numerous impaled corpses

Vocabulary

A. Circle the answer that fits best with the word in red.

1. sharp   pencil / ball / spoon

2. bite   hand / foot / mouth

3. original   first / last / second

4. claim   think / say / do

5. remind   remember / re-use / rest

6. execution   injure / kill / help

7. frightening   kitten / baby / wolf

8. gruesome   disgusting / pretty / stinky

9. stake   tire / pillow / stick

10. crack   water / road / sky

B. Place each expression in the correct sentence. You can use an expression more than once.

run down	suck out

1. I spilled my coffee, and it _____ the side of the table.

2. When I was bitten by a snake, my friend _____ the poison.

3. She bit the lemon and _____ the juice.

4. I dumped water on him and it _____ his face.

Which expression describes a liquid moving towards the ground? _____

Which expression describes a liquid being taken away? _____

Reading Comprehension

A. Main Ideas. Circle the answer that best completes each statement.

1. Vampires are monsters that _____ .

    a. impale their victims   **b.** suck blood from necks of people

2. Vlad the Impaler was _____ .

    a. a frightening vampire   **b.** a terrible ruler

3. Bram Stoker _____ .

    a. was inspired by the story of Vlad the Impaler
    b. described Vlad's terrible executions in his book, Dracula

B. Details. Write True or False after each statement.

1. Vampires can transform into many different animals.   _____

2. Vlad the Impaler was stronger than 20 men.   _____

3. Dracula was a character in Bram Stoker's book.   _____

4. Vlad the Impaler killed vampires with sharpened stakes.   _____

5. Vlad's nickname came from his method of execution.   _____

C. Inferences. Decide which of the statements can be inferred from the passage. Check the correct answers. (Choose two.)

_____ **1.** Many people were terrified of Vlad the Impaler.

_____ **2.** Bram Stoker got his idea for Dracula from a movie.

_____ **3.** Vlad the Impaler ruled for many years.

_____ **4.** The story of Dracula is scary for many children.

Writing

A. Organize. Write each answer (a-i) in the correct place in the chart.

Vlad the Impaler   Bram Stoker's Dracula

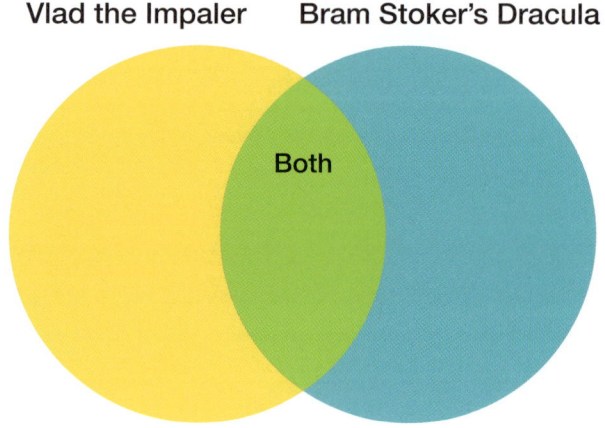

Both

a. impaled his victims
b. a terrible killer
c. a character in a book
d. a real person
e. sucked blood from his victims
f. can squeeze through tiny cracks
g. nicknamed for how he killed his victims
h. became the inspiration for a book
i. can turn you into a vampire

B. Synthesize. Use the information from Organize above to complete the advertisement for a documentary about Vlad the Impaler.

The True Story of Dracula

Dracula was real, and his name was _____ _____ _____ .

He wasn't a _____, but he was a terrible killer.

"Dracula" was nicknamed for how he _____ his victims, by _____ them on stakes.

Watch and learn how this frightening ruler became the _____ for Bram Stoker's famous book, Dracula.

Guesswork

Discuss your answers to these questions with your classmates.

1. How does this statue make you feel?

2. Do you think this is a real or imaginary creature?

3. What kinds of things might this creature do?

RH1-18
MP3

▲ Silver Bridge collapse (1967)

▲ **The Silver Memorial Bridge** The Silver Bridge collapsed in 1967; this bridge was completed in 1969 to replace the original Silver Bridge.

Too Scary to Help?

One cold evening in December, 1967, tragedy struck Point Pleasant, Ohio. The Silver Bridge suddenly collapsed, sending cars and people into the icy water below. Because it was rush hour, the bridge was full of cars. Most sank to the bottom of the river, taking their passengers with them. For months, the people of Point Pleasant talked about the disaster. But there was another, darker, topic of conversation as well. The Mothman was on their minds.

In the year leading up to the Silver Bridge disaster, a strange creature was seen all around Point Pleasant. The

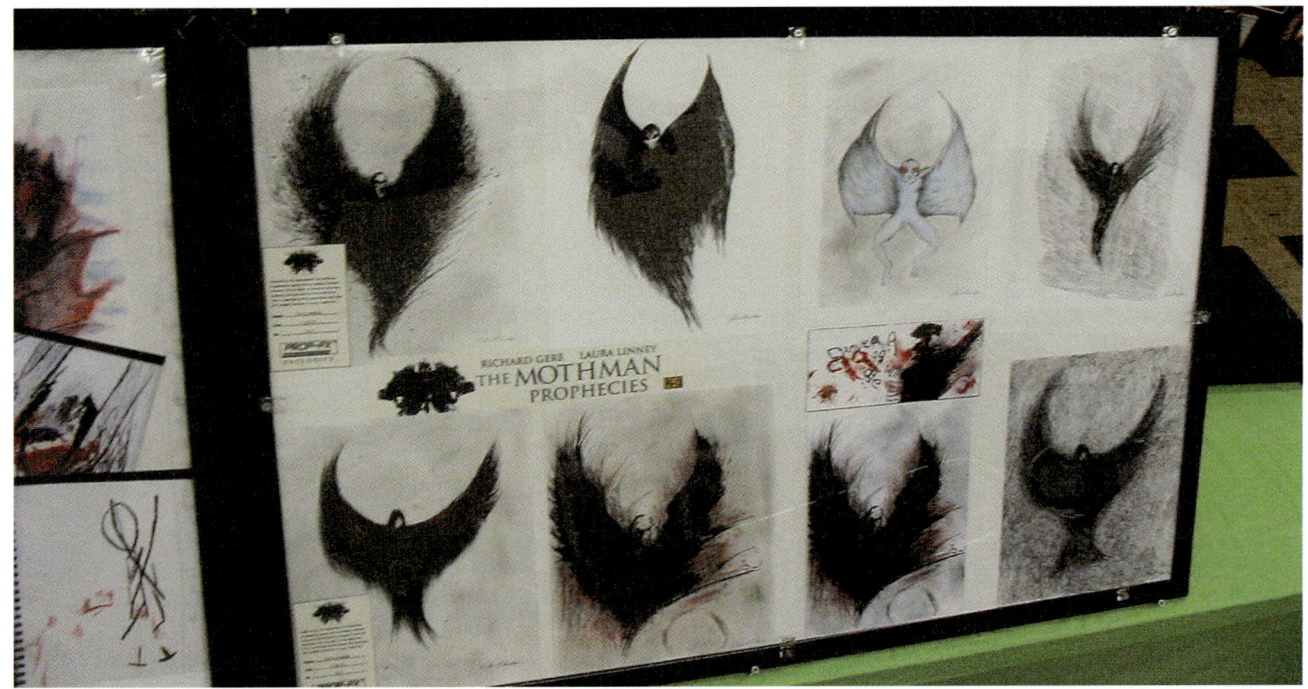

▲ **Mothman Museum, Point Pleasant** Many people describe the Mothman as having large red glowing eyes and looking like a man. Others describe a stranger creature, with eyes set in its chest.

people named it the Mothman because it looked like a tall man with giant, moth-like wings. It was gray and hairy with glowing red eyes. One couple reported being chased by it while they were driving more than 100 mph.

Another time it walked onto someone's porch and looked into their window. Once, it was seen hovering over the Silver Bridge.

There are a number of theories about the Mothman. Some think it was just a strange-looking bird or a big trick. Others claim that the Mothman was real. Some even think he was trying to warn the people of Point Pleasant about the upcoming Silver Bridge disaster. Maybe they are right. After the bridge collapsed, the Mothman was never seen again.

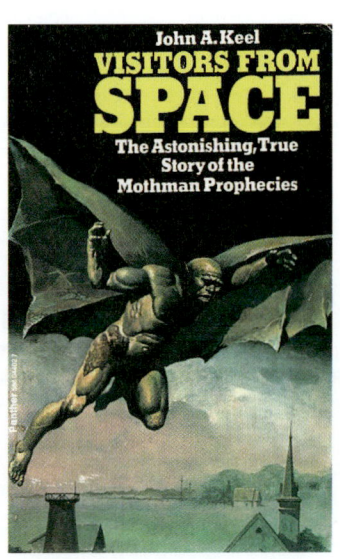

▲ The Mothman Prophecies was written by a journalist who experienced the Mothman sightings in person. Later, a movie was made of his book.

Vocabulary

A. Answer the questions in complete sentences. The first one has been done for you.

1. The loss of princess Diana was a great tragedy. Was it sad or happy?

It was sad.

2. My block tower collapsed when my brother kicked it. Did it fall down or stay up?

_____

3. I dropped my watch and it sank to the bottom of the pool. Did it rise or fall?

_____

4. There were too many passengers on the bus. Were there too many packages or people?

_____

5. I looked under the bed and I saw my cat's eyes glowing in the dark. Were they lit up or dark?

_____

6. The dragonfly hovered over my head. Was it still or moving?

_____

B. Fill in the blanks using the expressions from the box.

leading up to	a number of	on my mind	topic of conversation

1. In the weeks _____ my exam I was very nervous and stressed out.

2. I'm glad you called. You were _____ .

3. I get bored with Tom. Comic books are his only _____ .

4. There are _____ reasons that I want to quit. You are one of them.

Reading Comprehension

A. Main Ideas. Circle the correct answer for each question.

1. What is this passage mainly about?

    a. a horrible disaster

    b. a series of strange events

    c. the mystery of a deadly creature

    d. a strange-looking bird that looked like a monster

2. Which word best describes the Mothman?

    a. intelligent   **b.** helpful

    c. dangerous   **d.** mysterious

B. Details. Circle the answers that best complete each statement.

1. (1) _____ the Silver Bridge disaster, the Mothman (2) _____ .

(1) **a.** Years before   **b.** After   **c.** During

(2) **a.** was never seen again   **b.** appeared many times   **c.** caused great damage

2. Some people think that (1) _____ tried to stop (2) _____ .

(1) **a.** the Mothman   **b.** a trick   **c.** strange-looking bird

(2) **a.** the Silver Bridge disaster   **b.** the topic of conversation   **c.** rush hour

C. Inferences. Decide which of the statements can be inferred from the passage. Check the correct answers. (Choose two.)

_____ **1.** The Mothman caused the Silver Bridge disaster.

_____ **2.** The Mothman has been seen all over the world.

_____ **3.** Many people died during the Silver Bridge disaster.

_____ **4.** Not everyone believes the Mothman was real.

Writing

A. Organize. Write each statement in the correct box.

- Some think it was trying to warn people about the Silver Bridge disaster.
- Point Pleasant, Ohio
- They saw it flying, and one couple said that it chased them.
- A mysterious moth-like creature

WHERE did it happen?

_____

_____

_____

WHAT is the story about?

_____

_____

_____

EVENT or topic

"The Mothman"

HOW did people know about it?

_____

_____

WHY did it come?

_____

_____

_____

B. Synthesize. Use the information from Organize above to fill in the blanks of the advertisement for the Mothman festival.

The Mothman Festival

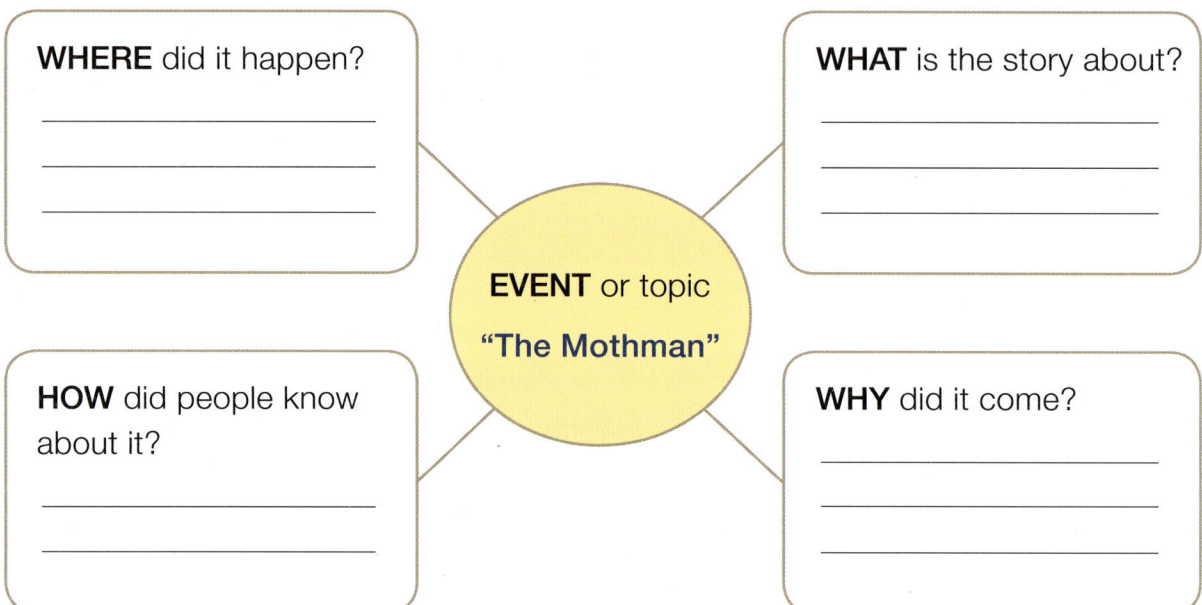

When: November 16th, 17th

The Mothman appeared around Point Pleasant for one year before the _____ _____ _____ in 1967.

Did he know it was going to happen?

Was he trying to _____ people?

Join us and celebrate this mysterious _____ creature.

Hear the story of a couple that say the Mothman _____ them in their car!

112

URASIAN PLATE

NORTH AMERICAN PLATE

EURASIAN PLATE

JUAN DE FUCA PLATE

CARIBBEAN PLATE

ARABIAN PLATE

PHILIPPINE PLATE

INDIAN PLATE

COCOS PLATE

EQUATOR

19

UNIT

AUSTRALIAN PLATE

PACIFIC PLATE

NAZCA PLATE

SOUTH AMERICAN PLATE

AFRICAN PLATE

AUSTRALIAN PLATE

SCOTIA PLATE

ANTARCTIC PLATE

The Ground Beneath Your Feet

Guesswork

Discuss your answers to these questions with your classmates.

1. What do you think this picture shows?

2. Count the plates. How many are there?

3. Are the plates the same as the *continents? Can you see any patterns?

*continent A major body of land surrounded by water. There are 7 continents on Earth.

▲ **Tectonic plates at Thingvellir National Park in Iceland** This huge rift is where the tectonic plates that form the Americas and Eurasia have shifted.

RH1-19
MP3

The Ground Beneath Your Feet

Did you know that the ground is moving? You can't usually feel it, but every day the ground moves. The earth is not solid. Far down beneath the land there is a great ocean of hot, fluid-like rock. We are actually floating on top of it.

The ground beneath our feet is the top layer of the earth. It may seem thick to us, but it is actually the thinnest of the layers. It is not one whole piece either. There are 8 major sections and dozens of smaller ones. They are called tectonic plates. Each plate moves on its own. They don't move that fast, though. The fastest plates usually move as fast as your hair grows!

We don't notice this slow movement, but the plates don't always move that slow. Sometimes they move as much as 10 meters at once. When two plates grind against each other, they can get stuck. They try to keep moving, though. Over time pressure builds and builds until SNAP! The plates jump forward. This sends shock waves out across the land and through the earth. It's an earthquake.

Earthquakes are most common in places where tectonic plates meet. In other places earthquakes can be quite rare. You might never feel the ground move, but if you do you'd better be ready for it.

▲ A big earthquake can send shock waves all the way to the other side of the planet.

▲ The hot, fluid-like rock under the tectonic plates is called magma. Sometimes it bubbles up to the surface, making a volcano.

▲ Because of the movement of tectonic plates, scientists have determined that at several different points in history, all of the land on Earth was combined together in one great supercontinent.

Vocabulary

A. Circle the answer that fits best with the word in red.

1. solid   rock / water / air

2. float   in / on / under

3. beneath   below / above / beside

4. whole   all / part / some

5. major   boring / interesting / important

6. notice   see / speak / touch

7. tectonic plate wet / tall / flat

8. grind   smooth / easy / rough

9. stuck   trapped / freed / cleared

10. pressure   loose / tight / light

B. Draw lines to make correct sentences. Write the completed sentences below.

1. She drove   •   • when she tied her shoes •   • Canada.

2. She was proud   •   • on top of   •   • on her own.

3. She put strawberries •   • all the way across   •   • the cake.

(1) She drove _____

(2) She was proud _____

(3) She puts strawberries _____

Reading Comprehension

A. Main Ideas. Complete the statement by circling the correct choice for each blank.

The passage is mainly about the **1.** _____ of **2.** _____ . So the main idea is that **3.** _____ .

1. **a.** movement   **b.** pressure

2. **a.** the ocean of hot, fluid-like rock   **b.** the top layer of the earth

3. **a.** tectonic plates move around on top of an ocean of hot fluid-like rock
     b. the fluid-like rock creates great pressure on the top layer of the earth

B. Details. Write True or False after each statement.

1. The earth is solid.   _____

2. The tectonic plates are all connected together.   _____

3. There are more than 30 tectonic plates.   _____

4. The fastest plates usually move quite slowly.   _____

5. When tectonic plates get stuck, they stop moving forever.   _____

6. When plates move quickly, it causes an earthquake.   _____

C. Inferences. Read each statement and decide if you think it is likely or unlikely. Check the appropriate box.

	Likely	Unlikely
1. Some tectonic plates are much bigger than others.	☐	☐
2. Earthquakes are impossible to stop.	☐	☐
3. Riding the tectonic plates is a popular sport in some places.	☐	☐
4. Every city in the world experiences at least one earthquake a month.	☐	☐

Writing

A. Organize. Look at the outline of the main ideas in the passage. Use the list of details to fill in the blanks.

- Sudden movement sends shock waves across the earth.
- The ground is made of pieces called tectonic plates.
- Tectonic plates float on top of an ocean of fluid-like rock.
- Pressure builds until the plates suddenly jump forward.

OUTLINE	
Main Ideas	**Details**
1. The ground moves a tiny bit every day.	a. _____ _____ b. _____ _____
2. When tectonic plates move quickly, it causes an earthquake.	a. Plates grind against each other and become stuck. b. _____ _____ c. _____ _____

B. Synthesize. Use the chart in Organize above. Fill in the blanks of the diagram with the correct information.

An earthquake in Three Stages

1. _____ _____ grind against each other and become _____ .

2. _____ builds until the plates suddenly jump _____ .

3. This sudden movement sends _____ _____ across the earth.

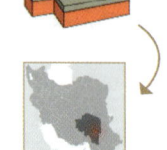

20

Almost Gone

Guesswork

Discuss your answers to these questions with your classmates.

1. Does this look dangerous? Why?

2. What is happening in the picture?

3. What part of an eruption do you think is the most deadly?

▲ Lake Toba is the crater lake resulting from the Toba event.

Almost Gone

▲ **Illustration of what the eruption might have looked like**
The Toba eruption caused a volcanic winter. Ash remained suspended in the air, blocking sunlight for close to 10 years.

Sumatra

Many species of animals are endangered. Their habitats have been destroyed and they are slowly disappearing. Mankind is to blame for much of this. But did you know that humanity was once endangered as well? We didn't do it to ourselves. It was because of a volcano.

Between 69,000 and 77,000 years ago, there was a great explosion at what is now Lake Toba in Sumatra, Indonesia. It was one of the largest volcanic eruptions in the history of the world. Geologists know this from looking at ancient layers of earth. They found a 15 centimeter thick layer of ash that once covered the whole of South Asia. It could only be from a massive eruption.

15 centimeters might not seem like much, but it was enough to kill almost every living thing in South Asia. The ash blocked sunlight from reaching plants, and those plants died. With their food source gone, many animals started dying as well, including humans. At that point in time, most ancient humans lived in South Asia. Thus, the effect on the human population was dramatic.

Scientists think there were only a few thousand humans left after the disaster. And only about 2,000 of them could have babies. We've come a long way since then. There are over 6.8 billion humans on Earth now!

▲ Some scientists believe that the Toba eruption may have triggered the most recent ice age.

Vocabulary

A. Answer the questions in complete sentences. The first one has been done for you.

1. The tiger is an endangered animal. Is it rare or common?

It is rare.

2. Eucalyptus forests are the Koala's main habitat. Are they the Koala's food or its home?

_____

3. Geologists can sometimes predict volcanic eruptions. Do they study the earth or the sky?

_____

4. My dog is massive. Is it really small or really big?

_____

5. I reached the mountain before dinner. Did I arrive at or leave the mountain?

_____

6. The bridge collapse was a dramatic event. Was it boring or impressive?

_____

B. Choose the answer closest in meaning to the underlined part of the sentence.

1. Ben wanted to marry me, but at that point in time, I was not ready to get married.

a. right then   **b.** later

2. In the past, people traveled on horses. We've come a long way since then.

a. improved greatly   **b.** gotten worse

3. Everyone agreed that Bill was to blame for the accident.

a. injured in   **b.** the cause of

Reading Comprehension

A. Main Ideas. Circle the correct answer for each question.

1. Why was humanity once endangered?

    a. Because we destroyed our habitat.
    b. Because of a volcanic eruption.

2. What part of the eruption was the most deadly?

    a. the ash
    b. the explosion

B. Details. Write True or False after each statement.

1. Only about 2,000 humans were left after the Toba disaster.   _____

2. The Toba event occurred tens of thousands of years ago.   _____

3. The ash killed plants by blocking the sunlight.   _____

4. Scientists know about the explosion from the bodies of dead animals.   _____

5. The humans that died all lived in the same area.   _____

6. All of the humans that survived could have babies.   _____

C. Inferences. Decide which of the statements can be inferred from the passage. Check the correct answers. (Choose one.)

_____ **1.** The ash was the only part of the eruption that was deadly.

_____ **2.** Natural disasters almost always cause species of animals to become endangered.

_____ **3.** Other species of animals became endangered after the Toba event.

_____ **4.** Some of the ash from the eruption traveled to North America.

Writing

A. **Organize.** Arrange the history of the Toba event in the correct order.

	Plants start dying.
	Ash falls over the whole of South Asia.
1	A volcano erupts near Lake Toba between 69,000 and 77,000 years ago.
	The human population is reduced to a few thousand.
	Animals start dying, including humans.

B. **Synthesize.** Using Organize above, complete the missing information in this depiction of a volcanic eruption.

1. A_____ is sent into the air.

2. The ash floats in the sky, b_____ sunlight.

3. The ash falls on p_____ and they start d_____ .

CREDITS

Notes

Notes

Enriching the Mind through Intriguing Learning-Oriented Readings

Reading Highlights

1

Workbook

WorldCom Edu

Reading Highlights

1

Workbook

WorldCom Edu

What's in a Head?

Words & Expressions

A. Choose the correct definition for each word below.

behead	perch	accident	expect	survive

1. _____ : an event that happens by mistake
2. _____ : to cut off a creature's head
3. _____ : a high place for birds to sit and sleep
4. _____ : to think that something will happen
5. _____ : to stay alive

B. Choose the word that best completes each sentence.

1. Are you _____ your backpack? Someone left one in the classroom.

   a. beheading   **b.** swinging   **c.** missing   **d.** expecting

2. I only needed three drops of water, so I used a(n) _____ .

   a. axe   **b.** eyedropper   **c.** menu   **d.** tour

3. Did you _____ weight over the winter? You look bigger.

   a. expect   **b.** gain   **c.** survive   **d.** peck

C. Fill in the blanks using the expressions from the box.

pick out	take a bath	chop off

1. Be careful with that axe. I don't want you to _____ a finger!
2. Can you help me _____ a pair of shoes? I just can't decide.
3. You stink! Please _____ .

Summary

D. Complete the summary with the correct words.

chopped	head	tours	survived	eyedropper

"Miracle Mike" was a chicken who lived without a _____ for one and a half years. A farmer _____ his head off, but Mike _____ . The farmer was amazed so he kept Mike alive by feeding him with an _____ . The Farmer took Mike on _____ around the country and made thousands of dollars.

Writing

E. Unscramble the words and write them in the blanks.

1. still alive / he / to find Mike / and pecking / woke up

_____ .

2. and corn / Farmer Olsen / to feed milk / used an eyedropper / into Mike's neck

_____ .

3. Mike / so well / gained 5 pounds / that he even / ate

_____ .

F. Look at the picture and answer the questions.

1. What is missing in the picture?

➡ _____ .

2. Is this a drawing of a real or imaginary person?

➡ _____ .

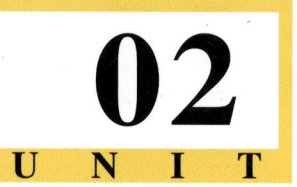

Above and Beyond

U N I T

Words & Expressions

A. Choose the correct definition for each word below.

| record | best-selling | copyright | argue | professional |

1. _____ : a law that protects a book, movie, or song from being copied

2. _____ : having a record for selling many copies

3. _____ : to disagree and to talk about the disagreement

4. _____ : a measurement of something that is great

5. _____ : acting and looking like a serious worker

B. Choose the word that best completes each sentence.

1. Can you help me _____ my book? It's an exciting mystery about dolphins.

   a. argue   **b.** set   **c.** publish   **d.** agree

2. Our school has a great _____ . He lets the teachers play movies in class!

   a. argument   **b.** director   **c.** record   **d.** talent

3. Why is that movie so _____ ? I thought it was long and boring.

   a. popular   **b.** curious   **c.** agreeable   **d.** professional

C. Fill in the blanks using the expressions from the box.

| at first | set a world record | give it away |

1. I'm going to _____ for sneezing the most times in one minute!

2. I didn't like him _____ , but now we are best friends!

3. Don't throw old stuff in the trash. You should _____ to people who need it.

Summary

D. Complete the summary with the correct words.

agree	hunting trip	answer	world record	argument

The Guinness Book of World Records can tell you about almost any _____ . Sir Hugh Beaver got the idea for the book on a _____ . He had an _____ with the other hunters about which bird was faster, the golden plover or the grouse. They couldn't _____ , and Hugh couldn't find the _____ in any book, so he suggested that Guinness make a book of world records.

Writing

E. Unscramble the words and write them in the blanks.

1. the largest / do you know / sandwich / is / how big / in the world

_____ ?

2. was faster / he and the other hunters / started / which bird / arguing about

_____ .

3. he / be done / that something / decided / had to

_____ .

F. Look at the picture and answer the questions. Use the hint in the parenthesis.

1. What are the men doing? [a world record]

→ _____ for the biggest paper airplane.

2. What world record do you want to set?

→ I want to _____ .

5

Words & Expressions

A. Choose the correct definition for each word below.

fog	torch	village	cliff	theory

1. _____ : a high wall of rock
2. _____ : water in the air that makes it hard to see
3. _____ : a stick that burns and gives light
4. _____ : a small and simple kind of city
5. _____ : an idea about how something happens

B. Choose the word that best completes each sentence.

1. There's a _____ kind of apple that I like. It's green and a little sour.

   a. various   **b.** certain   **c.** few   **d.** many

2. Were you _____ in class today, too? I didn't understand anything!

   a. mysterious   **b.** superstitious   **c.** patient   **d.** confused

3. I think I gained weight. My jeans _____ fit!

   a. easily   **b.** barely   **c.** smartly   **d.** smoothly

C. Fill in the blanks using the expressions from the box.

no one knows	fall out of	pick up

1. Your camera is going to _____ your pocket if you're not careful.
2. The car keys are missing again, and _____ where they are!
3. You should _____ your backpack. It's going to get wet if you leave it on the ground.

Summary

D. Complete the summary with the correct words.

superstitious	confused	fog	fall	spirits

Every fall, birds _____ from the sky over the village of Jatinga. Ancient villagers thought the birds were _____ sent from the sky, but modern villagers aren't _____ . They even eat the birds. Some people think that the birds fall because they are _____ by the dark and the _____ , but that doesn't explain why birds don't fall in similar places all over the world.

Writing

E. Unscramble the words and write them in the blanks.

1. birds mysteriously / from the sky / on certain dark / fall / and foggy nights,

_____ .

2. and the darkness / he / for food / was perfect / was looking

_____ .

3. were spirits / early villagers thought / sent from the sky / that the birds / to scare them

_____ .

F. Look at the picture and answer the questions.

1. Describe the bird in the picture.

➡ _____ .

2. Do you think this is a picture of a modern or ancient bird?

➡ _____ .

04 A Flying Trap

Words & Expressions

A. Choose the correct definition for each word below.

prey	notice	powerful	helpless	backwards

1. _____ : very strong

2. _____ : animals that are hunted

3. _____ : moving towards the back

4. _____ : unable to do anything

5. _____ : to see or hear something

B. Choose the word that best completes each sentence.

1. It's too cold outside; you should _____ your head or you might get sick.

    a. form   **b.** feed   **c.** cover   **d.** catch

2. I like that painting. Could I _____ it on my wall?

    a. notice   **b.** hang   **c.** help   **d.** rise

3. I dug a deep hole and put a rabbit in it. It's a tiger _____ !

    a. trap   **b.** tail   **c.** insect   **d.** direction

C. Fill in the blanks using the expressions from the box.

sort of	has no use for	take a close look at

1. Can you _____ my essay? I want to know if it is written well.

2. Blair already has a bike. She _____ another one.

3. Brian's cat is big and orange. It looks _____ like a fox.

8

Summary

D. Complete the summary with the correct words.

catch	colored	hairs	walking	directions

Dragonflies are brightly _____ and have big wings. Their wings let them fly in many different _____ . Dragonflies can travel 50 to 60 miles per hour. A dragonfly's legs are not used for _____ . Instead, a dragonfly uses its legs to _____ prey. Its legs have small _____ which help trap insects.

Writing

E. Unscramble the words and write them in the blanks.

1. and brightly colored / their big wings / make them / bodies / easy to spot

_____ .

2. its big wings / the first things/ are / you'll notice

_____ .

3. a dragonfly has / wings, / you might think / no use / with such powerful / for legs

_____ .

F. Look at the picture and answer the questions. Use the hint in the parenthesis.

1. Is the dragonfly easy to spot? Why? [brightly colored]

➡ _____ .

2. What is the dragonfly doing? [stick]

➡ _____ .

A Different Kind of Brain

Words & Expressions

A. Choose the correct definition for each word below.

skill	social	button	title	confidence

1. _____ : the name of a book or a movie

2. _____ : a round piece that holds cloth together

3. _____ : having to do with other people

4. _____ : an ability

5. _____ : belief that one is strong

B. Choose the word that best completes each sentence.

1. That is a very _____ sort of apple. It only grows in France.

    a. common   **b.** social   **c.** skilled   **d.** rare

2. I have a lot more _____ now that I speak English well.

    a. confidence   **b.** buttons   **c.** miracles   **d.** diseases

3. How many English words did you _____? I can remember 5,000 words.

    a. combine   **b.** memorize   **c.** flee   **d.** bathe

C. Fill in the blanks using the expressions from the box.

at least	go up to	in person

1. You own _____ 20 different pairs of shoes. Do you really need more?

2. Brittany Spears is my favorite singer. I'd love to meet her _____.

3. I don't like to _____ strangers and ask for directions.

Summary

D. Complete the summary with the correct words.

social skills	memorized	newspaper	disease	strangers

Kim Peek was born with a _____ that made some things difficult. He couldn't button his own shirts and he was slow to learn _____ . But the disease also gave Peek an incredible memory. He _____ every word of at least 12,000 books over his lifetime. He also amazed _____ by telling them what stories were in the _____ on the day that they were born.

Writing

E. Unscramble the words and write them in the blanks.

1. he could / every word of / at least / remember / 12,000 different books

_____ .

2. many important / he / to learn / social skills / was also slow

_____ .

3. he'd read / with each eye / at once, / one page / two pages

_____ .

F. Look at the pictures and answer the question. Use the hint in the parenthesis.

Q. How does the actor that played Kim Peek look different from him? [Glasses]

➡ _____

_____ .

11

Words & Expressions

A. Choose the correct definition for each word below.

entire	exist	legend	normal	appear

1. _____ : an old fictional story
2. _____ : to look like something
3. _____ : average, not different or strange
4. _____ : to be real
5. _____ : complete

B. Choose the word that best completes each sentence.

1. Help! My dog was just attacked by a _____ bear!

    a. entire   **b.** bloodthirsty   **c.** mythical   **d.** gentle

2. I am _____ going to the party. I love dressing like a pirate!

    a. slightly   **b.** definitely   **c.** mostly   **d.** originally

3. There is a _____ tonight. Everything is so bright!

    a. full moon   **b.** cage   **c.** circus-goer   **d.** beast

C. Fill in the blanks using the expressions from the box.

instead of	most of the time	from head to toe

1. _____ I ride the bus, but sometimes I like to walk.
2. She fell in the pond and when she got up she was covered _____ in mud!
3. Can we eat pizza _____ lasagna for dinner tonight?

12

Summary

D. Complete the summary with the correct words.

origins	suffer	circus	remove	beasts

The legend of werewolves has its _____ in a real disease called hypertrichosis. The disease causes people to grow long hair all over their bodies. The people aren't _____ , but they look like them. In the past, these people had trouble finding work and often ended up in the _____ . Now modern science can _____ their hair so they don't have to _____ anymore.

Writing

E. Unscramble the words and write them in the blanks.

1. terrible / when the moon / something / is full, / happens

_____ .

2. the legend / its origins in / of the werewolf / truth / may have

_____ .

3. have the hair / most people / can just / removed / with werewolf syndrome

_____ .

F. Look at the picture and rearrange the words to make a complete sentence.

Q. Describe the picture.
[a long beard / The lady / has / and long hair]

➡ _____

_____ .

Reach for the Sky

Words & Expressions

A. Choose the correct definition for each word below.

arrest	strap	realize	worry	childhood

1. _____ : to tie down strongly
2. _____ : to put in jail
3. _____ : to suddenly know
4. _____ : to think about something bad happening
5. _____ : the time when someone is a child

B. Choose the word that best completes each sentence.

1. When I released the balloon, it _____ high into the sky.

   a. snapped   **b.** realized   **c.** worried   **d.** floated

2. I'm going to have a party in my _____. I mowed the lawn and even bought a pool!

   a. runway   **b.** weather balloon   **c.** eyesight   **d.** backyard

3. My brother was _____ for driving too fast last night.

   a. packed   **b.** arrested   **c.** wondered   **d.** decided

C. Fill in the blanks using the expressions from the box.

give it a try	took to the sky	because of

1. I've never jumped from a plane, but I'd like to _____.
2. _____ the snow storm, school was cancelled today.
3. We were going faster and faster, and then suddenly we _____!

Summary

D. Complete the summary with the correct words.

lawn chair	floated	runway	tied	pilot

Larry Walters dreamed of being a _____ , but couldn't be one because he couldn't see well. He never forgot about flying, though, and one day he took to the skies in a _____ . He _____ 45 weather balloons to it and _____ to 15,000 feet. He flew over an airport _____ , so he shot some balloons and floated to the ground.

Writing

E. Unscramble the words and write them in the blanks.

1. could lift / wondered / if they / into the sky / him / he

_____ .

2. and he was / he / strapped himself / off / into the chair,

_____ .

3. a few balloons / floating down / with his pellet gun, / he shot / and started slowly

_____ .

F. Look at the picture and answer the question.

Q. Are the balloons strong enough to lift a person?
   (Answer in a complete sentence.)

➡ _____

   _____ .

Words & Expressions

A. Choose the correct definition for each word below.

vibrate	bath	dry	jet	imaginable

1. _____ : possible to imagine
2. _____ : to take all water away from
3. _____ : a container filled with water for cleaning
4. _____ : to move very quickly back and forth
5. _____ : fast moving air

B. Choose the word that best completes each sentence.

1. Here, _____ my belly right here and you can feel the baby.

   a. vibrate   **b.** dress   **c.** press   **d.** spend

2. Yesterday my phone _____ in my pocket and it really scared me.

   a. lifted   **b.** spent   **c.** vibrated   **d.** dressed

3. My mother takes _____ naps. She sleeps for one hour every afternoon.

   a. imaginable   **b.** regular   **c.** human   **d.** forever

C. Fill in the blanks using the expressions from the box.

feel like	there's no need	takes time

1. You have to be patient. Getting a passport _____ .
2. Calm down. _____ for violence.
3. You should try this new coffee. It will make you _____ a bird.

Summary

D. Complete the summary with the correct words.

sound	jets	dry	button	human

The ultrasonic bath is a _____ washing machine. It's as simple as climbing in and pressing a _____ . The ultrasonic bath will clean and _____ you in less than 15 minutes. It uses _____ to vibrate the dirt right off of you. Then it uses _____ of hot air to dry you.

Writing

E. Unscramble the words and write them in the blanks.

1. people / hours a day / would spend / their things / cleaning

_____ .

2. you / and press / into the machine / just climb / a button

_____ .

3. have you / a building / thunder / shake / ever seen

_____ ?

F. Look at the picture and answer the questions. Use the hint in the parenthesis.

1. Where is the woman? [Ultrasonic Bath]

➡ _____ .

2. What do you think the machine in the picture is used for? [clean]

➡ _____ .

17

Ghost Hunter

Words & Expressions

A. Choose the correct definition for each word below.

thermometer	weapon	equipment	expertise	capture

1. _____ : great knowledge of a certain subject
2. _____ : tools used for a certain job
3. _____ : a tool used to hurt or kill animals or people
4. _____ : a tool used to tell how hot or cold it is
5. _____ : to catch and hold

B. Choose the word that best completes each sentence.

1. Here, _____ onto that branch and climb into the tree.

   a. capture   **b.** advance   **c.** grab   **d.** detect

2. My computer is a(n) _____ device. Please don't get it wet.

   a. expert   **b.** electronic   **c.** haunted   **d.** invisible

3. That English textbook is too _____ for these students. We should use a different book.

   a. invisible   **b.** advanced   **c.** electronic   **d.** haunted

C. Fill in the blanks using the expressions from the box.

all sorts of	next time	show up

1. It's ok if you wear your shoes now, but _____ please take them off.
2. I love going to the market. There are _____ strange smells, sights and sounds.
3. You should _____ to school at least 10 minutes before class starts.

Summary

D. Complete the summary with the correct words.

| invisible | show up | cold spots | kill | pictures |

Ghost hunters don't _____ ghosts, they find them. Ghosts are _____, so ghost hunters use specialized equipment to detect them. Thermometers are used to detect _____ and cameras are used to take _____ of ghosts. Even though you can't see ghosts, they sometimes _____ in pictures.

Writing

E. Unscramble the words and write them in the blanks.

1. all sorts of / professional ghost hunters / haunted places / will take you / to explore

_____.

2. ghost hunters / find ghosts / many different ideas / about how to / have

_____.

3. pictures of ghosts / of all kinds / cameras / are used / to capture

_____.

F. Look at the picture and answer the questions.

1. Look at the picture and describe your feelings about it.

➡ _____.

2. Is this ghost young or old?

➡ _____.

10 Did You See That?

Words & Expressions

A. Choose the correct definition for each word below.

government	object	investigate	report	saucer

1. _____ : a thing
2. _____ : a flattened sphere
3. _____ : to say that you heard or saw something
4. _____ : an organization that runs a country or city
5. _____ : to find information about a topic

B. Choose the word that best completes each sentence.

1. You like pizza? You should join our pizza-eating _____!

   a. organization **b.** government **c.** sighting **d.** evidence

2. You always tell me that candy is bad for me, but what is your _____?

   a. field **b.** evidence **c.** fiction **d.** report

3. Please _____ your clothes into lights and darks.

   a. research **b.** concern **c.** separate **d.** investigate

C. Fill in the blanks using the expressions from the box.

across the country	concerned about	nobody knows

1. I've asked all my friends, but _____ where my shoes are!
2. I became _____ the storm after it knocked down a tree near my house.
3. People _____ are coming together to celebrate Christmas.

Summary

D. Complete the summary with the correct words.

UFO	organization	proof	sightings	reported

Ufology is the study of UFOs. A _____ is anything a person sees flying in the sky, but can't identify. People _____ seeing so many UFOs that the government became worried and started an _____ to investigate these _____ . Because there wasn't much _____ , the government doesn't support ufology anymore. But ufology is still a popular field of study.

Writing

E. Unscramble the words and write them in the blanks.

1. of UFOs / about increasing / the US government / reports / became concerned

_____ .

2. sure / or not / if UFOs were / they weren't / real

_____ .

3. who saw it / of a UFO sighting / is / the story of / the person / the only evidence

_____ .

F. Look at the picture and answer the questions.

1. What do you think the object in the picture is?

➡ _____ .

2. Describe the shape of it. What does it look like?

➡ _____ .

City of Ghosts

Words & Expressions

A. Choose the correct definition for each word below.

clever	marry	temple	forbid	catch

1. _____ : to not allow something
2. _____ : smart and practical
3. _____ : to legally agree to live forever with another person
4. _____ : to see or find someone doing something
5. _____ : a place for practicing religion

B. Choose the word that best completes each sentence.

1. I can't believe that you ate a(n) _____ pizza in 10 minutes!

   a. clever   **b.** local   **c.** empty   **d.** entire

2. Jim and I work together to write a _____ newspaper. It's mostly for our friends.

   a. local   **b.** cursed   **c.** abandoned   **d.** ruined

3. The farmers say that a witch _____ their cows and now they won't give milk.

   a. cursed   **b.** crushed   **c.** rolled   **d.** threw

C. Fill in the blanks using the expressions from the box.

shortly afterwards	rolled away	fell in love with

1. I dropped my ball and it _____ down the hill.
2. I blew the whistle, and _____ my dog came running.
3. The prince _____ a beautiful girl, but she was not a princess!

Summary

D. Complete the summary with the correct words.

| legend | haunted | sunset | forbids | ruins |

Bhangarh is an abandoned city located in Rajasthan, India. Locals claim that it is
_____ . They say that they hear music coming from the _____ after
dark. For this reason the government _____ anyone from entering the city
between _____ and sunrise. _____ claims the city was cursed by an
evil magician who fell in love with a beautiful princess.

Writing

E. Unscramble the words and write them in the blanks.

1. Bhangarh / they / from entering / and sunrise / forbid anyone / between sunset

_____ .

2. that would make / he made / the princess / an evil potion / come to him

_____ .

3. rolled away, / and crushed him / the magician, / right onto / the rock

_____ .

F. Look at the picture and answer the questions.

1. How does the haunted house make you feel?

➡ _____ .

2. What do you think is inside the house?

➡ I think _____ .

23

Living in a Maze

Words & Expressions

A. Choose the correct definition for each word below.

| alley | rooftop | rule | located | lawless |

1. _____ : in a certain area
2. _____ : to control
3. _____ : having no rules
4. _____ : a pathway between buildings
5. _____ : the very top of a building

B. Choose the word that best completes each sentence.

1. A repairman is coming tonight to _____ my new washing machine.

   a. remain   **b.** rule   **c.** install   **d.** decide

2. I used to be a(n) _____ of that apartment building, but I moved after it caught on fire.

   a. builder   **b.** officer   **c.** criminal   **d.** resident

3. Pammy draws great _____. Many are too hard for me to solve!

   a. governments   **b.** responsibilities   **c.** mazes   **d.** alleys

C. Fill in the blanks using the expressions from the box.

| add onto | torn down | for this reason |

1. We're going to _____ our house this fall.
2. My cat is very loud at night. _____ we keep her in the basement.
3. Last year, the old middle school was _____ and a new one was built.

Summary

D. Complete the summary with the correct words.

government	decided	densest	criminals	connected

Kowloon Walled City was a small area of Hong Kong that did not have a _____ .
It grew on its own into one of the _____ areas ever. Without rules, residents
added onto the city however they wanted. Passageways _____ most of the
buildings. There were too many _____ inside the city, so the Hong Kong
government _____ to demolish it.

Writing

E. Unscramble the words and write them in the blanks.

1. nor China / took / for it / neither Britain / responsibility

_____ .

2. they wanted / people / onto the city / added / however

_____ .

3. these "roads" were / got almost / so dense / no sunlight / that the lower alleys

_____ .

F. Look at the picture and answer the questions. Use the word in the parenthesis.

1. What is this a picture of?

➡ It is _____ .

2. Why is a maze difficult? [passageways]

➡ It is difficult because _____ .

To Be an Astronaut

Words & Expressions

A. Choose the correct definition for each word below.

space shuttle	guide	challenge	prepare	astronaut

1. _____ : a person who travels in space
2. _____ : a vehicle that travels in space
3. _____ : to get ready for something
4. _____ : a very difficult task
5. _____ : to help something move in a certain direction

B. Choose the word that best completes each sentence.

1. I asked my father and my mother, but _____ one will say yes.

   a. both   **b.** either   **c.** neither   **d.** every

2. You need to wear a special _____ when you go sky-diving.

   a. food   **b.** suit   **c.** course   **d.** challenge

3. Have you ever _____ a hurricane? They are so awesome!

   a. trained   **b.** built   **c.** experienced   **d.** prepared

C. Fill in the blanks using the expressions from the box.

designed to	focus on	at the controls

1. Hop into the tractor. I'll sit in the back and you sit _____ .
2. My new shirt is _____ keep me warm in cold weather and cool in hot weather.
3. You just need to _____ your studies. Then you will do well on the test.

Summary

D. Complete the summary with the correct words.

| suits | prepares | machines | weightlessness | simulated |

At Space Camp, campers train just like real astronauts. They wear the same
_____ , eat the same food, and even use the same _____ as real
astronauts. They can even experience _____ . There are different courses, and
each course _____ the camper for a unique job in the final challenge of space
camp — a _____ space shuttle flight.

Writing

E. Unscramble the words and write them in the blanks.

1. imagine / to be an astronaut / what it's / can you / like

_____ ?

2. real astronauts / train / boys and girls / just like / from around the world

_____ .

3. they / campers / can / focus on / choose / what

_____ .

F. Read the question and arrange the words into a complete and correct answer.

Q. What is happening in the picture?
[coming / are / from / the bottom of / the rocket]

➡ Bright flames _____ .

27

Words & Expressions

A. Choose the correct definition for each word below.

oxygen	conduct	limited	maintain	station

1. _____ : a place used for a special or official purpose
2. _____ : to keep something working
3. _____ : the part of air that keeps us alive
4. _____ : not going beyond a certain point or amount
5. _____ : to do in an official or purposeful way

B. Choose the word that best completes each sentence.

1. Some basketball players can jump so high that it looks like they can beat _____ .

   a. toothpaste   b. stations   c. gravity   d. oxygen

2. The dog cannot come inside until somebody _____ the mud off of him.

   a. breathes   b. exercises   c. saves   d. rinses

3. Most restaurants only last for a short time, but I think mine will be a _____ success.

   a. long-term   b. limited   c. difficult   d. weightless

C. Fill in the blanks using the expressions from the box.

in the middle of	take care of	on board

1. Can you help me _____ my brothers tonight? I'll give you 10 dollars.
2. Sometimes my mom puts cheese _____ the burgers. It is delicious.
3. You should always give up your seat to elderly people _____ the train.

Summary

D. Complete the summary with the correct words.

experiments	limited	nations	travel	weightless

People from over 15 _____ have lived in space on board the International Space Station. Scientists use the ISS to do _____ and to learn about more long-term space _____ . Living on the ISS isn't easy. Being _____ is challenging for the body, and many important things are _____ in space.

Writing

E. Unscramble the words and write them in the blanks.

1. and take care of / the space station / in the ISS / astronauts staying / conduct experiments

_____ .

2. that are / simple / in space / on Earth / are difficult / many things

_____ .

3. special machines / breathable / clean the air / and make it

_____ .

F. Read the question and arrange the words into a complete and correct answer.

Q. What is the astronaut doing?
[taking / is / he / the space station / care of]

➡ _____
_____ .

Making Music

Words & Expressions

A. Choose the correct definition for each word below.

bowstring	shaped	evolve	electricity	speaker

1. _____ : a thin line that is connected to a bow

2. _____ : having the shape of

3. _____ : an electronic device used to make sound

4. _____ : to change over time

5. _____ : the movement of electrons

B. Choose the word that best completes each sentence.

1. I like cookies that are _____ like hearts.

    a. common   **b.** stringed   **c.** electric   **d.** shaped

2. I like the _____ that a guitar makes. It has a soft but clear sound.

    a. guitar   **b.** speaker   **c.** shape   **d.** twang

3. The upright bass is one of the largest _____ instruments.

    a. stringed   **b.** shaped   **c.** pleasant   **d.** common

C. Fill in the blanks using the expressions from the box.

go further	at the bottom of	pull back

1. Sometimes you can find prizes _____ a cereal box.

2. Every year people _____ into the world of mobile technology.

3. Put your foot on the clutch, and then _____ on this lever.

Summary

D. Complete the summary with the correct words.

hunting bows	instruments	boxes	bowstring	snap

Modern guitars probably have their origins in ancient _____ . When a _____ is pulled back and released, it will _____ forward and make a pleasant twang. The first record of ancient stringed _____ shows a bow harp. The bow harp is shaped just like a hunting bow, but has many strings. _____ were added to these first stringed instruments, and they eventually developed into the modern guitar.

Writing

E. Unscramble the words and write them in the blanks.

1. pulls the bowstring / and releases it / his bow, / back / he picks up

_____ .

2. stringed instrument / to show up / the bow harp / is the first / in ancient art

_____ .

3. to make / electric guitars / their sound big / use speakers

_____ .

F. Read the question and arrange the words into a complete and correct answer.

Q. What is this a carving of?
[playing / a man / bow harp / the]

➡ It is a carving of _____ .

31

Playing with Food

Words & Expressions

A. Choose the correct definition for each word below.

cucumber	creative	drill	performance	improvise

1. _____ : a show

2. _____ : a tool used for making holes

3. _____ : new and interesting

4. _____ : to do without planning

5. _____ : a long, green, juicy vegetable

B. Choose the word that best completes each sentence.

1. You should work _____ 12, and then go to bed.

    a. under   **b.** during   **c.** until   **d.** after

2. People carve scary faces into _____ for Halloween.

    a. cucumbers   **b.** meals   **c.** members   **d.** pumpkins

3. Could you _____ some of your soup with me? I'm still hungry.

    a. share   **b.** transform   **c.** create   **d.** improvise

C. Fill in the blanks using the expressions from the box.

at the end of	have you ever	sounds like

1. All of the children shouted and laughed _____ the school day.

2. _____ eaten the green part of a watermelon?

3. Did you hear that? It _____ a monkey is in your closet.

Summary

D. Complete the summary with the correct words.

audience	drills	instruments	performers	soup

The Vienna Vegetable Orchestra uses vegetables to play music. The _____
are interested in all kinds of art and music. They make their _____ using
_____ and knives, just hours before the performance. Their music is
improvised, and each performance is unique. After the show, the instruments are
cooked into a _____ and eaten by the performers and the _____ .

Writing

E. Unscramble the words and write them in the blanks.

1. music and art / in different kinds of / each performer / is interested

_____ .

2. and made / are bought / the instruments / each performance / just hours before

_____ .

3. there are / for each one / and new music / new instruments

_____ .

F. Read the question and arrange the words into a complete and correct answer.

Q. How do you play the cucumber recorder?
[mouth / with / you / it / play / your]

➡ _____ .

17 A Terrible Monster

Words & Expressions

A. Choose the correct definition for each word below.

| horrible | inspire | victim | squeeze | enemy |

1. _____ : to make smaller by pressing
2. _____ : someone who suffers
3. _____ : to help create an idea
4. _____ : someone whom you fight against
5. _____ : very bad

B. Choose the word that best completes each sentence.

1. My pencil needs to be _____ . It's too dull.

    a. reminded   **b.** inspired   **c.** sharpened   **d.** frightened

2. I don't have any _____ because I am kind to everyone I meet.

    a. executions   **b.** stakes   **c.** claims   **d.** enemies

3. Your book _____ me to change my life. Now I am a doctor!

    a. inspired   **b.** claimed   **c.** squeezed   **d.** bit

C. Fill in the blanks using the expressions from the box.

| suck out | follow the rules | ran down |

1. Everyone tells me to _____ , but I don't understand why I need to.
2. Do you like to _____ the seeds from a pomegranate?
3. The river flooded and _____ the street.

Summary

D. Complete the summary with the correct words.

killed	nicknamed	frightening	sharpened	inspired

Vampires are _____ , blood-sucking monsters, and Dracula is the scariest of all. The character, created by Bram Stoker, was _____ by a real person named Vlad the Impaler. Vlad's real last name was Dracula, but he was _____ "the Impaler" because of the way that he _____ his enemies. He impaled them on _____ stakes, and they died slowly and very painfully.

Writing

E. Unscramble the words and write them in the blanks.

1. he uses / to bite / your blood / and suck out / your neck / two sharp teeth

_____ .

2. because of / nicknamed / his enemies / "the Impaler" / how he killed / Vlad was

_____ .

3. Vlad / for days / the dead bodies / hanging / would leave

_____ .

F. Look at the picture and answer the questions. Use the words in the parenthesis.

1. Describe the picture. [blood, neck]

➡ A vampire _____ .

2. How does this picture make you feel?

➡ _____ .

Too Scary to Help?

Words & Expressions

A. Choose the correct definition for each word below.

disaster	chase	hover	rush hour	warn

1. _____ : a great and horrible event
2. _____ : to fly without moving
3. _____ : a time of day when there are many travelers
4. _____ : to tell someone about a future danger
5. _____ : to run after someone or something

B. Choose the word that best completes each sentence.

1. Because I am so _____ , my friends nicknamed me "the Gorilla."

   a. glowing   **b.** hairy   **c.** upcoming   **d.** icy

2. I like to sit on the _____ and listen to the wind blow.

   a. porch   **b.** tragedy   **c.** theory   **d.** passenger

3. I am excited for the _____ alien movie. It is supposed to be really scary!

   a. upcoming   **b.** hairy   **c.** glowing   **d.** icy

C. Fill in the blanks using the expressions from the box.

leading up to	on her mind	a number of

1. Mariah looks distracted. She must have something _____ .
2. In the year _____ my marriage I worked to save a lot of money.
3. I own _____ expensive cars. Buying them is my hobby.

Summary

D. Complete the summary with the correct words.

| creature | red eyes | collapsed | disaster | moth-like |

In December, 1967 the Silver Bridge _____ in Point Pleasant Ohio. In the year leading up to its collapse, a strange _____ was seen around Point Pleasant. It was hairy and grey, with big, _____ wings and great glowing _____ . After the bridge collapsed, the Mothman was never seen again. Some people think it was trying to warn everyone about the upcoming _____ !

Writing

E. Unscramble the words and write them in the blanks.

1. cars and people / suddenly collapsed, / into the icy water below / sending / the Silver Bridge

_____ .

2. seen / over the Silver Bridge / it was / hovering

_____ .

3. the Mothman / after the bridge / again / collapsed, / was never seen

_____ .

F. Look at the picture and answer the question.

Q. What is happening in the picture?

➡ _____

_____ .

The Ground Beneath Your Feet

Words & Expressions

A. Choose the correct definition for each word below.

shockwave	earthquake	grind	section	snap

1. _____ : when the ground moves suddenly
2. _____ : the sound made when something breaks
3. _____ : energy released by an explosion or sudden movement
4. _____ : a part of a whole
5. _____ : to move against roughly

B. Choose the word that best completes each sentence.

1. This cake has three _____ : chocolate, vanilla and strawberry.

   a. fluids   **b.** layers   **c.** tectonic plates   **d.** shock waves

2. Look! A cat is _____ in that tree. Someone call the fire department.

   a. noticed   **b.** floating   **c.** grinding   **d.** stuck

3. There was too much _____ in the hose, so it exploded.

   a. pressure   **b.** shockwaves   **c.** plates   **d.** sections

C. Fill in the blanks using the expressions from the box.

all the way	dozens of	on your own

1. I picked up my shoe and _____ ants came crawling out!
2. I can't believe my dog walked _____ home from California!
3. You need to do your homework _____ . I'm not going to help you anymore.

Summary

D. Complete the summary with the correct words.

stuck	float	ocean	earthquake	layer

The earth is not solid. Under the thin top _____ of the earth, there is a great
_____ of hot fluid-like rock. The top layer is made of tectonic plates that
_____ on this ocean. The tectonic plates usually move very slowly. When they
get _____ together, pressure builds up. When there is too much pressure,
they move suddenly and cause an _____ .

Writing

E. Unscramble the words and write them in the blanks.

1. the ground / of the earth / our feet / is / beneath / the top layer

_____ .

2. the fastest plates /grows/ usually move / as your hair / as fast

_____ .

3. they can / grind / when two plates / get stuck / against each other,

_____ .

F. Look at the picture and answer the question. Use the hint in the parenthesis.

Q. What does the picture show? **[the inside]**

➡ _____

_____ .

Almost Gone

Words & Expressions

A. Choose the correct definition for each word below.

| dramatic | ancient | ash | population | mankind |

1. _____ : every human together as a group
2. _____ : very old
3. _____ : what is left over after something burns
4. _____ : a number of living beings in a certain place
5. _____ : very noticeable and surprising; impressive

B. Choose the word that best completes each sentence.

1. _____ has discovered incredible things and changed the world.

   a. Disaster   **b.** Ash   **c.** Humanity   **d.** Species

2. People have created new _____ of plants and animals.

   a. mankind   **b.** eruptions   **c.** species   **d.** disasters

3. My winter coat is nice and _____ . It keeps me very warm.

   a. ancient   **b.** thick   **c.** endangered   **d.** dramatic

C. Fill in the blanks using the expressions from the box.

| come a long way | at that point in time | to blame for |

1. Our school used to have more students. _____ we had fewer teachers too!
2. My brother used to eat crayons. He's _____ since then.
3. I think John is _____ the accident. He was driving too fast.

Summary

D. Complete the summary with the correct words.

erupted	endangered	reduced	thick	living thing

Tens of thousands of years ago a volcano _____ near Lake Toba, in Indonesia. It was one of the largest volcanic eruptions in history. A _____ layer of ash fell over the whole of South Asia, killing almost every _____ there. The human population was _____ to a few thousand, making mankind an _____ species.

Writing

E. Unscramble the words and write them in the blanks.

1. slowly disappearing / their habitats have / and they are / been destroyed

_____ .

2. that humanity / endangered / was once / did you know / as well

_____ ?

3. sunlight / from reaching / and those plants / the ash blocked / died / plants,

_____ .

F. Look at the picture and answer the questions. Use the word in the parenthesis.

1. What does this picture show? [volcanic]

➡ _____ .

2. What is in the air?

➡ _____ .

Reading Highlights

Reading Highlights is a three-book reading comprehension series for intermediate learners of English as a foreign language. Intriguing and stimulating content is delivered through a series of approachable and well-organized passages. The clarity and natural feel of the writing encourages students to engage the text with an inquisitive mind. Students are guided towards the discovery that written English can be fun and relevant to their lives and interests.

Key Features:

* Colorful and Engaging graphics that present the material in an eye-catching way
* Vocabulary exercises that lead students from reviewing the unit vocabulary to practicing and expanding their use of it
* Comprehension exercises that test understanding and encourage an investigative approach to reading
* Organize exercises that provide a framework for students to re-state and re-organize passage content
* Synthesize exercises that help students recall passage content in a new way

Components

* **Student Book / Workbook**

Download resources at **www.wcbooks.co.kr**
MP3 files / Word lists / Translations with answer keys / Test sheets

Reading Highlights Series

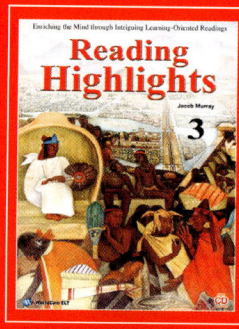

WorldCom Edu   www.wcbooks.co.kr